CATASTROPHE IN THE PACIFIC

The sub, cruising at snorkel depth, was in the process of charging its main batteries. Somewhere in the vent system, either because of human error or a minor malfunction, the normal operating procedure broke down and a small amount of hydrogen was trapped in a confined area. Over a period of time, the pressure in this area increased, due to the continual inflow of this odourless, colourless gas, and the vapour spread to fill ever greater space. Something, a spark or simply a hot spot near an exhaust manifold, ignited this flammable gas and, in its confined condition, it immediately and without warning blasted into an incandescent cloud.

The Jennifer Project

CLYDE W. BURLESON

SPHERE BOOKS LIMITED
30/32 Gray's Inn Road, London WC16 8JL

Original American edition published by
Prentice-Hall Inc., Englewood Cliffs, New Jersey, USA 1977

Copyright © Clyde W. Burleson 1977

Published by Sphere Books Limited 1979

TRADE MARK

Set in Monotype Garamond

Printed in Great Britain by
C. Nicholls & Company Ltd
The Philips Park Press, Manchester

INTRODUCTION

The art and science of gathering information about one's friends and enemies have been complicated by the advances of modern technology.

And in the process, a lot of glamour has gone out of the business. It's hard to compare the image of a silk-wrapped, voluptuous Mata Hari, whirling in time to the cacophonous wails of Near Eastern music and promising a thousand and one delights, with twenty people sitting in a huge room listening over earphones to Chinese radio broadcasts and making notes. Or ten people carefully clipping and cross-filing stories from Yugoslavian newspapers printed in Cyrillic characters.

But the efficiency of a modern intelligence operation, which uses computers to organize millions of bits of data and comes up with meaningful information, is greater than any one person's ability to coax secrets from a susceptible member of the opposite sex by pillow talk.

Experts state there are eight modern spy shops in the world. America has one; as do the Russians, the English, the French, the West Germans, the Japanese, the Israelis and the Red Chinese. They also tell us America's is the most mechanized. Many people think the term *mechanized*, as applied to the business of spying, means trick cars, gimmick briefcases, and fountain pens which shoot bullets, take pictures, or record voices. And it's true, some of this gadgetry does exist, but intelligence gathering today is mostly dependent upon more global devices.

Every civilised country in the world disseminates enormous amounts of information about its problems, infra-structure, and every other facet of its socio-politico-economic activities. This on-going, daily outpouring of endless, seemingly random data is monitored and electronically sorted by intelligence services.

There are also the amazing electromechanical spy devices. Satellites circle the globe, covering every mile of the earth's surface in a selected number of revolutions. They receive and send signals, and are used in navigation, communications, legitimate scientific explorations and, of course, plain old peeking and spying.

But as well observed as the earth is from above, this surveillance is almost nothing compared to the equipment installed below, in the oceans. Intelligence gathering has become a technician's dream, and an old-time, out-in-the-cold spy's nightmare.

Certainly, there is still room for the field operative. A CIA officer, for example, stationed in Mozambique with a network of agents in South Africa, could produce many 'bits' to be entered into the computer matrix. But his role is constantly being minimized.

Far and away the greater concentration of manpower engaged in the gathering of information on the clandestine and public activities of other nations is in the technical areas of surveillance. At times, it's a routine sort of work, because each individual is feeding only a part of the whole into the machines. And it's the same kind of part, day after day. A lot of the old-time action and glamour have gone out of the business and have been replaced by a new kind of teamwork.

So it's no wonder when an occasional technical project with some inherent romance does come along there is a lot of interest and enthusiastic support from the intelligence community. Project Jennifer, which in its later stages became Project Azorian, was just such an operation. From a technical standpoint, it was matchless. Somehow, in some way, using the furthest fringes of man's technological achievements, a sunken Soviet submarine was to be recovered from the bottom of the Pacific Ocean from a depth of more than three miles. The very concept was almost unimaginable, and reeked of science fiction. It would require the combined application of the best engineering minds in America to have even a chance of success.

And the project wasn't bad from the cloak-and-dagger side either. More than 4,000 people would be called upon to work on some portion of the secret project before the operation was complete. There would be adventure on the high seas, just the right amount of risk to the physical well-being of the participants and finally, the lure of money – up to $500 million, according to many reports, for a single operation bringing together many of the best features of the old world of spying with the new ones of intelligence collection and interpretation.

It would be a great adventure. The story of how it came about, how it was carried out, what was found and how its still-unsettled elements are causing yet-to-be-felt ripples in our system is worth telling. At times, it's hard to keep it from sounding like fiction.

The combination of Howard Hughes, the CIA, satellites, ships sailing on secret missions, complex cover stories, sophisticated electronic undersea listening devices, interdepartmental wars inside the U.S. government, threats by outside political forces, just the right amount of personal danger – all combine to make the affair seem most unlikely. But the reality is there, backed by facts. By any standard, it's an epic tale of one of the most astonishing achievements of mankind.

On another level, the story is also something more. The unravelling of the complex tangle of people, places, times and events and the sorting of these elements into an ordered whole provide a unique insight into the workings of both the CIA and the U.S. Government. Private citizens are not often offered a view into the inside of a classified operation while it is still timely. Usually, such revelations occur only when the event is outdated history. In this instance, however, a window has been opened on a contemporary scene. The vista it offers is a panoramic view of government in action and a close-up of the complexity of a modern spy operation.

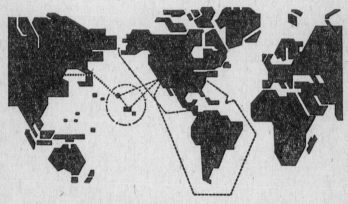

Path of the Hughes Glomar Explorer ●–●–●–●–●
Path of the Soviet Sub ●●●●●●●
Area Covered by Sea-Spider ──●──●──●

On an almost direct line with the northern border of Korea, the Murav'yev-Amurskiy peninsula juts from the Siberian body of Mother Russia into the dark cold waters of the Sea of Japan. At the southern end of this peninsula is the city of Vladivostok. Its location is no accident; it is on a well-protected bay, the Zolotoy Rog or Golden Horn. One of the best natural deep-sea harbours in the world, completely sheltered from the violent vicissitudes of nature, the Golden Horn is a natural resource which has made the area the main Soviet naval base on the Pacific since 1872.

Located far enough north so ice breakers are frequently needed to keep the port open, Vladivostok's climate in the winter months is less than hospitable. Dawn comes late and the sky is a constant dull grey. As often as not, a misty overcast shrouds the more than four kilometers of quays and ship berths.

Following the contours of the Horn on the end closest to the chill waters of the Sea of Japan, construction has been completed on a series of rough concrete slips. And on any given day, several long, black, whale shapes ride almost motionless in the lapping swells of the oil-slicked water.

Since the Soviets have the largest armada of submarines in the world, these pens are seldom empty, and sudden arrivals and departures of both nuclear and diesel-powered vessels are an almost unnoticed everyday experience.

There are nicer ports from which to sail, and when the klaxon reverberates with shocking clarity through one of the huge boats, the crew is probably looking forward to being snugly below and well away from the dreary harbour. Thanks to the location they can be quickly obliged. Once the boat comes alive, vibrating as the engines begin to generate power, it can slide, submerged, into the Sea of Japan in a matter of minutes.

Seen from the surface, a sub under way is a breath-taking sight. Its round wet shape moves silently through cresting seas, trailing a long, white wake. Appearing to be more alive than mechanical, it slips lower and lower into the water, until a final wave washes upon nothing, and the boat is gone from the world of man. It has become a temporary visitor with limited licence in a hostile kingdom.

The sailing of another 'Golf'-class sub in February 1968 received only routine notice. Unlike some of her more exotic, nuclear-powered sisters, she was an older, diesel-engined craft. There were at least twenty more of her style in the fleet, and their whale shapes, topped by an exaggeratedly large 'fin' or 'sail,' were a common enough sight.

Her departure was normal. As was the almost instant U.S. satellite surveillance report which noted her sailing, and was routinely submitted, along with other comings, goings, and position reports, to a division of the Office of Anti-Submarine Warfare and Ocean Surveillance, United States Navy.

It was an ordinary beginning for a very unusual voyage.

The 'G' or 'Golf'-class series of boat first came to life in the Soviet shipyards of Komsomolsk and Severodvinsk in 1958, the year the United States was building its last diesel-powered sub. At that time she represented the latest Soviet thinking in sub-surface craft design.

Russian interest in undersea vessels was, and still is, intense, partly because of the memory of the German sub fleet and its successes during World War II. Immediately following the end of hostilities in Europe, and in violation of international laws prohibiting any nation from salvaging another's warships, the U.S.S.R. set a precedent by claiming several German subs equipped with the 'snorkel' underwater breathing apparatus, which had made the U-boat a practical and feared weapon.

The snorkel is an interesting and seemingly simple device. It allows exhaust gases from the huge diesel engines, used to charge the batteries supplying propulsion to the vessel, to pass into the atmosphere while the ship is travelling at periscope depth underwater. A separate system is used to vent the ship of the hydrogen and chlorine gases formed by chemical reactions as the batteries charge and discharge.

One of the early problems of submarine design was the development of a power system that would work under water. The internal combustion engine was ruled out since it would use up all available oxygen on board the ship in a matter of minutes, and the officers and crew would die, most unpleasantly, of asphyxiation. The only other choice of power then available was the electric motor. It was clean and non-polluting to operate, but required a constant supply of electric energy. A combination of the two power sources proved to be the answer. A large diesel-type engine was connected to an electric generator. On the surface, the diesel operated normally, using outside air to power the generator, which produced enough electricity to turn the huge electric motor used for propulsion and to build a charge in a series of storage batteries. Once submerged, the diesel engine was shut down and the electric motor drew on the power stored in the batteries to provide operating speed.

The main drawback was not the complexity of the

system, because it was quite reliable, but the necessity of surfacing every few hours to run the diesel and recharge the banks of batteries. And, at the same time, exhaust the ship of all traces of the highly explosive and deadly poisonous hydrogen and chlorine gases, produced by chemical reactions inside the batteries.

A submarine on the surface is an excellent target. Designed for swiftness in the depths, a sub cannot be fitted out as an effective surface warship. It must depend upon stealth, not absolute fire power, for its victories.

Snorkel breathing did away with much of the need for surfacing, and constant improvements in the system by both the Soviets and the U.S. Navy resulted in vessels capable of running for days at depths of twenty to thirty feet.

All basic snorkel design, including the first installation of the device into ships of the line, was of German origin. At the end of World War II, the Allies moved their intelligence people into this area of research as soon as possible. So we all started with about the same technological base.

The Soviets, however, placed a greater emphasis on conventional diesel-electric boats, while America developed the first atomic-powered vessels. This has resulted in the Russians having a far larger sub fleet than does the United States. But the U.S. sub packs have a dominant position from the standpoint of speed and range. Estimates of the Soviet fleet in the 1960's indicated the U.S.S.R. had more than 525 operational submarines. Today that number has grown to more than 720. It's easy to compare this to the Nazi fleet of 440 U-boats, but it must be remembered the Nazi vessels were not all operative at the same time.

The 'G'-class sub is a far cry from World War II undersea craft. Not only is it larger (a 'Golf'-class boat displaces 2,800 tons submerged; the biggest U-boats scaled out at about 2,100 tons), it's faster, more manoeuvrable and better armed. Capable of a speed of 17 knots, this class of boat has an operational surface cruising range of more than 20,000 miles; less than her atomic sisters (with displacements over 5,000 tons) but enough to remain an effective delivery force for nuclear weaponry. A 'Golf'-class boat is designed around the conventional double hull and probably is operational to depths of about 500 feet. She originally carried ten 21-inch torpedo tubes, six in the bow and four in the stern.

But the unique and visible feature of the ship is the rather bulbous, tall fin or sail, designed to house three missile launchers. The 'Golf'-class submarine was originally built for the missile system designated as the SS-N-4, capable of firing the 350-mile-range Sark missiles. Starting in 1967, many of the boats in this class were updated by replacing the SS-N-4 system with the SS-N-5. The newer system allows the improved Serb missile to be fired from a partially submerged position, and deliver a 1-megaton nuclear warhead to targets as far as 700 miles away. The conversion, first performed on the nuclear 'Hotel'-class boats, has apparently proved very successful, making the 'G' series an extremely effective weapons platform.

Several of these modified boats were assigned to the submarine pens at Vladivostok and, as first-rate ships of the line, are used to patrol the North Pacific and the Sea of Japan.

No U.S. source is certain about the mission assignment of the 'G'-class sub which left Vladivostok on that dismal morning, but her course has been well established. Once clear of the Sea of Japan, she sailed a straight path with few deviations, making good speed through the open, rolling waters of the North Pacific.

Her initial detection and subsequent surveillance were carried out by a unique system of spy-in-the-sky satellites, working in computer-harnessed combination with an amazing undersea surveillance system, used by the United States to cover about one-third of the total sea area of the Pacific, as well as portions of the Atlantic, the Caribbean, the eastern Mediterranean and the North Sea, and the coasts of Portugal, Turkey, Britain, Denmark, Tunisia, Sicily and Sardinia.

Effective thought and planning for this undersea network first began in the 1950's, influenced by the successful installation of the unmanned early-warning radar stations known as the 'Dew Line.' These completely automated facilities, strung in a line through the Arctic region of North America, provided the earliest possible warning of a flight of bombers or missiles coming at the United States via the North Pole.

The 50's were the years of the strategic aircraft in the popular press, but while our eyes were on the sky the real contest was shaping up under water. Nuclear-powered, missile-carrying submarines had been discussed in engineering circles for years. In the U.S., Adm. Hyman G. Rickover and his task force were close to operational with their first designs for such vessels.

It was apparent the nuclear sub, with its almost limitless range and capacity for staying submerged and undetected, would produce serious problems in the balance of power if some means were not found to track and account for them.

The 1955 launching of the first Inter-Continental Ballistic Missile (ICBM)-carrying, atomic-powered sub, *USS Nautilus*, named for Jules Verne's science fiction craft, gave the undersea detection problem new importance. The hypothetical need became one of immediate reality. In a short time, both Soviet and U.S. military accepted the atomic sub. As the newest weapon of war, it became a major component in combat planning.

With necessity as a stimulus, several projects, including the then top-secret 'Caesar,' an early, fixed-position underwater listening and detection system, were started, to explore different approaches to the problem of ongoing submarine surveillance. This intensive preliminary work led, during the Kennedy Administration, to the formation of the National Reconnaissance Office (NRO), which was assigned responsibility for all research, development and procurement of U.S. satellites and other aerial intelligence programmes. The NRO operated undercover in both the Air Force and the Navy and played a strong role in the eventual success of U.S. undersea detection programmes.

As the surveillance system functions today, the initial contact phase of tracking is handled by special satellites launched from a Pacific Coast site south of Los Angeles near Camp Cook, a World War II Army training ground. A list of satellite orbit insertions turns up a fascinating array of acronyms such as TIROS (Television Infrared Observation Satellite) and ITOS (Improved TIROS Operational Satellite). The same launch list enumerates almost countless space shots designed to insert into orbit a number of instrument packages labelled secret. And the secret designation has meant precisely that.

According to the Satellite Situation Report, compiled from data furnished by the Goddard Space Flight Centre, the Smithsonian Astrophysical Observatory and the North American Air Defence Command (NORAD), as of February 1976 more than 3,800 objects were in orbit, and there were almost 5,000 additional 'decayed' orbital items. (A 'decayed' item has an orbit showing progressive signs of allowing the object to fall back into the atmosphere of the earth.)

Numerous reports have been published concerning large pieces of odd-shaped metal dropping onto towns, woodlands and ships at sea. These random falling elements, some of considerable size, are a potential hazard, not because of the likelihood of their actually striking someone (the odds against such a happening are immense), but because they might appear on U.S. or Soviet early-warning radar screens and be interpreted as an ICBM re-entering the atmosphere. Such a 'bogey' could, say some experts, trigger a nervous officer into an action with potentially dire global consequences.

To counter this possibility, a constant effort is made to

17

predict the re-entry times and locations for all sizable pieces of space junk, and this information, developed by NORAD, is relayed through the Pentagon to its opposite numbers in the U.S.S.R. Hardly a day passes without a hefty hunk of burned-out metal falling back to the planet of its manufacture, and this continual monitoring effort is another remarkable facet of our complex atomic-military world.

The specific numbers, purpose and method of operation of America's very numerous spy satellites remain a closely guarded, highly classified matter. A few facts are, however, known. The use of infrared radiation as a ship-tracking device is a good example. At the time of this writing, there is in orbit a series of detectors capable of reporting to ground relay stations information on heat trails left in the ocean by various types of ships. This normally invisible telltale track lingers in the wake of a vessel for days, allowing a very accurate plot to be established by the computers to which the sensors high above the earth in orbits criss-crossing the globe have provided their reports. The system is able to identify the general type of vessel, as well as its power source.

Airborne television cameras are also known to be in service, as are sensors tuned to receive selected electro-magnetic wavelengths. Recent photos of the surface of Mars taken from Viking I and II unmanned landers show remarkable surface detail in computer-printed pictures electronically relayed to the earth. As good as these shots are, they are surpassed by the detail available from several earth-orbiting units. High resolution in this field is a direct result of the work by Hughes Aircraft in the design of signal-amplifying microwave tubes, only one of their many sky-spy contributions.

Although a spokesman from the U.S. Navy specifically refused to comment on the satellite tracking of the particular 'G'-class sub which was to instigate the Jennifer Project, answers given to other questions make it appear likely a track was detected by satellite sensors shortly

18

after the ship left the Sea of Japan. This early warning led to the monitoring of the vessel when she entered the web of the Sea Spider.

Little is known about the specifics of this gigantic under-water tracking system. That it is an outgrowth, along with several other installations, of the successful Project Caesar (1960-1962) is certain. Western Electric is the prime contractor for the equipment used in this detection network. The heart of the technique is the deployment, in a system called line and vertical array, of underwater microphones called hydrophones capable of relaying to a central source for computer display noises passing through the water. Contrary to reports in *The Los Angeles Times,* the U.S. is not alone in this field. While she is well advanced in the strategic use of these devices, the Soviets and others deploy similar systems designed for tactical purposes.

Hydrophones have been around since the 30's, and through the years, refinements have resulted in super-sophisticated units capable of converting a wide variety of subsurface sound waves into transmittable signals. When these units are deployed in a long line of precisely fixed geographic coordinates, they are capable of producing data which may be analysed to determine a ship's course, size and design. When the same instruments are strung vertically down into the depths, additional, almost three-dimensional information is produced.

Augmenting these sonic sensors are other devices tuned to detect heat waves and specific parts of the electro-magnetic spectrum. The data produced from all these various arrays, when fed into the right computer pro-gramme, yield a very clear picture of traffic in a given area.

The Pacific network extends outward from the U.S. coast for more than 1,300 miles on a line from the tip of Alaska south to the Baja, California, peninsula. An additional 1,300-mile circle rings the Hawaiian Islands.

The entire web of Sea Spider is the largest undersea

acoustic-detection system ever placed in operation, and its construction costs are estimated at about $1.5 billion.

Headquarters in the Pacific is on the island of Oahu, and continuous surveillance of all vessels in the 1,300-mile network is a matter of course. This strategic system, like its Atlantic counterpart, extends to a distance slightly greater than most known Soviet submarine-carried Intermediate Range Ballistic Missile (IRBM) ranges. The Soviet Golem II, a currently operational missile, has an effective shooting distance of 1,200 to 1,240 miles.

Within the hundreds of thousands of square miles monitored by this undersea surveillance network, all ship passages are noted. But special attention is given to submarines, and an extremely careful, untiring effort is made to follow every one passing within firing distance and penetrating the Sea Spider's web. All subsurface data, combined with information received from the orbiting satellites, are interpreted to develop profiles showing each submarine's direction of travel, speed, probable point of departure and operating depth.

A Soviet sub known to be a missile carrier is even more closely scrutinized, and special attention is focused on it if it should linger near its operational missile-firing depth. Accurate vectors can be instantly transmitted to anti-submarine attack vessels, surface missile ships and aircraft, to allow for combat strikes should the need arise.

The case of the 'G'-class sub that was the focus of the Jennifer Project is an excellent example of the efficiency of our total underwater surveillance system.

The vessel was detected as a possible web penetrator shortly after leaving port, and a computer-commanded electronic-watch file was set up on her in the Pacific head-quarters. When the first hydrophone contacts were made several days later, an entry vector into the surveillance area had already been computed, and as the early data arrived from the fringe-location hydrophones, a complete tabulation of her type, class, power, probable weaponry complement and other information was immediately available. At this point, the lock-on to the sub was complete, and electronic course plots were monitored by the computer banks.

Naturally, no sign of the silent web manifested itself to those on board the submerged vessel.

No one knows exactly what happened on board the ship. And it is very unlikely anyone will ever know.

The chronology of events probably is this:

The sub, cruising at snorkel depth, was in the process of charging its main batteries. Somewhere in the vent system, either because of human error or a minor malfunction, the normal operating procedure broke down and a small amount of hydrogen was trapped in a confined area. Over a period of time, the pressure in this area increased, due to the continual inflow of this odourless, colourless gas, and the vapour spread to fill ever greater space. Something, a spark or simply a hot spot near an exhaust manifold, ignited this flammable gas and, in its confined condition, it immediately and without warning blasted into an incandescent cloud.

A review of the reconstructed sounds gathered into the U.S. Navy's Pacific headquarters, combined with a general technical study of 'Golf'-class boats, indicates a venting problem is the most likely difficulty which could have caused a blast of such magnitude. The hydrogen gas given off during the charging cycle of the storage batteries is, when confined, both a powerful and highly volatile material.

An actual recording was produced of the sound made by the explosion, and the noises generated as the ship sank deeper and deeper. The implosion of the hull is a part of this gruesome record.

Inside the ship, the sound must have been like being closed in a steel garbage can with a string of exploding firecrackers. The first half-muffled bangs grunted and rattled their way through the confined spaces, and no

21

doubt brought looks of shock from the crewmen. The second, larger blast rocked the boat itself and spelled the end.

Stern hull plates were torn, released air and allowed tons of water to pour into the tail of the craft. The powerful diesels rocked to a stop. As the boat began to list rear end down, water gained access to the electrical power system, adding darkness to the terror of the stunned crew. As the angle of descent steepened, the smashing, clinking tinkle of breaking china and personal effects served as a cacophonous background to the dull thunk of bodies slamming into the solid-steel bulkheads.

In the command centre, the action was probably frantic and somewhat confused. One moment the sub was in a routine manoeuvre; the next, it had sailed into chaos.

Auxiliary lighting systems, providing a dim glow throughout the ship, must have snapped on, only to flicker and fail as the crew strove desperately to dump ballast and add power to stop their backward descent. But it was to no avail.

The single most shocking thing about the sinking is the rapidity with which the submarine nosed up and, falling backward, went out of control. Almost no deviation in her downward course has been reported, and she sank at an astonishing rate of speed. Inside, as the sub passed the designed hull depth, life ended quickly. The pressure of water, squirting from cracks in the steel sheet of the pressure hull, struck with killing force, crushing some of the men in their tracks. As the ship gained momentum and plunged deeper, seam after seam tore with a shrieking rending of thick metal, and the vessel began to develop a velocity never anticipated by her builders.

Falling ever faster, the sub started to twist and turn. A mile ... two ... three ... then a final jarring squelch, as she plowed into layers of prehistoric mush, sending gigantic sprays of primordial ooze upward and outward for thousands of yards. Slowly, like whirling streams of dust motes in still air, the heavier particles began to settle back, gradually returning to the black calmness of the depths.

Experts differ on the possible velocities a submarine may reach in an incident such as this, but speeds of up to a hundred miles per hour are not uncommon estimates. At this velocity, even allowing for a considerable layer of soft ooze and sediment, impact with the bottom is made with enormous force, comparable to a gigantic airliner crashing to ground.

Phenomenal damage is done to the structural integrity of the submarine, and each stress is magnified by the pressure from the dark surrounding waters which, three miles down, exceeds 7,000 pounds per square inch of surface.

There is virtually no way a submarine could remain intact under such conditions. Studies of the sites of two sunken U.S. Navy submarines, *Thresher* and *Scorpion*, indicate breakage of the boats into at least three components and metallic debris scattered over a wide area.

So the story of Project Jennifer starts with a paradox.

A Soviet submarine is detected and tracked by an amazing undersea network of highly sophisticated electronic gear. It runs into trouble, and due to an explosion, or rather a series of explosions on board, it sinks. The possibility of sabotage is almost nonexistent. The sub's position is clearly known to the U.S. Navy. It is lying there, in the timeless depths, with a cargo of 86 dead men, assorted nuclear weaponry, and an untold wealth of information from which a modern intelligence agency could derive valuable facts about another government's military capabilities and organization.

The submarine, according to experts, should be broken into pieces. Yet, later CIA reports of the Jennifer Project recovery activity indicated the 'Golf'-class vessel was intact, in one piece, on the bottom. No less an expert than Capt. William Walker, an engineer with the U.S. Navy's Office of the Oceanographer, is quoted by *Science* magazine as saying, 'I would have expected at least the bow and stern sections to have been fractured off.'

This vital discrepancy will arise again and again to cast doubt on every popular report concerning the Jennifer Project. And it becomes a major factor in understanding the phenomenal success of the entire operation.

2

Soviet activity in the days immediately after the disappearance of the sub followed their previously observed pattern. Every ship, in every Navy, has regularly scheduled times for making contact with higher command. This communications routine is so well established, in fact, as to cause immediate concern when a vessel fails to report as ordered. This is especially true in the case of a submarine, and even though there are more possible things to prevent an undersea boat from completing its contact schedule, the missing of a single designated radio response is guaranteed to attract attention.

As days passed, and still no word was received from the lost vessel, calls to the ship from various station locations were increased until a full 24-hour contact and response watch was in effect. The mission of the vanished sub must have been studied and reviewed, and all possible combinations of technical communications difficulties considered and rejected.

During March 1968, Soviet efforts to make contact with the sub became almost frantic. Fishing trawlers, long known to be special reconnaissance boats equipped with vast arrays of listening and detection devices, were dispatched from several ports to follow the projected course of the missing submarine and to search for floating debris and oil slicks, besides performing all normal electronic surveillance.

Radio broadcasts were doubled, then doubled again, and additional channels were placed on 'guard' to be monitored on a continuing basis aboard all Soviet vessels.

Since Soviet policy allows for no publicity on military disasters or accidents, no public announcement was made of the feared loss. Our intelligence reviews show no trace of a sunken-sub story in their press.

Finally, after weeks of futile attempts, the use of multi-channel broadcasts 'in the clear,' or without code, were instituted, in the apparent hope against hope some survivor, not familiar with the more advanced communications techniques, might respond to the language of his homeland. But the effort was for naught.

The trawlers plowed the seas, watching and listening, and recorded only miles of blank and empty ocean under endless blue skies. The radio messages, taped and repeated mechanically on an eternal replay, brought no response.

Slowly, the truth became unavoidable. The 'Golf'-class submarine, with her entire complement of officers and crew, was lost at sea, with the specific location of the disaster and the cause unknown. This was, as far as can be ascertained, the first peacetime loss of a Soviet submarine in which the ship totally disappeared without leaving its navy a clue to its final fate or resting place. Such a mysterious sinking wouldn't occur again until 1972, when a nuclear-powered 'November'-class boat, carrying three missiles, would vanish in the rough, cold seas 900 miles north of Newfoundland. No trace of this second vessel has ever been reported.

By May 1968, the efforts to contact the missing boat were winding down, and the close surveillance of all suspected disaster sites was relaxed. By the first of June, except for limited activity and final reports, the entire matter had become, as far as the Soviet Navy was concerned, another mystery of the deep.

The U.S. Navy, however, had different ideas entirely, based on more exact information. The hydrophone recordings provided by Sea Spider were ominously clear. By careful measurement of the recording traces, aided by computerized calculations, a very good fix had been made on the disaster site. As soon as was practical, the location was placed under aerial surveillance to determine if the Russians intended to carry out any deep salvage operations. The reactions of the Soviets were monitored, and their increasingly frequent radio transmissions as well as the prowling trawlers were carefully noted, but the Soviets overlooked the area to a great extent in their months of searching.

Realizing it had exclusive information, the U.S. Navy placed the results of the Sea Spider and satellite plots under tight security, and a high level of secrecy was clamped on all position-fix estimates. Several Soviet 'tries' to probe for any information the U.S. might possess about their missing boat were thwarted, and the extent of American knowledge was not revealed.

The rebuff had to be made with consummate care and skill, because the Russians possess more than a basic comprehension of our hydrophone network and are well aware of the constant monitoring of their ships as they pass through the designated control areas. No record is publicly available as to the number of inquiries made during this period, but there is no reason to assume other than normal efforts, which would include official requests for information to the Department of State and the Navy as well as cross diplomatic contacts and unofficial probing through members of the academic and scientific communities. Being experts at leaving few stones unturned, it is almost certain the Soviets also enlisted their usual number of international humanitarian organizations in this project, probably on the ground of the grief of the missing men's families.

There can be little doubt the Russians knew we had some information, but were unaware of the real extent of our knowledge.

The Navy held the line, and apparently there were no

leaks which either confirmed or denied our having information on the sunken vessel's fate or location.

The top-secret effort, which located the site in relation to the NAVSAT (for Navigational Satellite System), was confined to a very limited number of personnel, all of whom proved highly trustworthy. During this March to May period, the Navy continued its close watch on the Russian effort and was prepared to act as soon as the Soviet surveillance effort relaxed.

The opportunity came in June 1968. By mid-May, the Russians had abandoned their round-the-clock trawler fleet activity and were using only radio as a contact device; obviously a final effort. By early June, even the sporadic radio activity was finally silent.

After a brief wait, the U.S. Navy began to move, commencing an operation planned months before. The deep-sea reconnaissance ship USS *Mizar* was dispatched to the site indicated by the hydrophone data and NAVSAT coordinates.

Mizar is one of the most remarkable vessels in the U.S. Navy. More capable than her Soviet counterpart, *Vityaz*, she is in many ways one of the most unique ships in the world. In addition to highly sophisticated radio gear, *Mizar*, dubbed an Oceanographic and Research vessel, is equipped with the absolutely latest sonar capabilities, facilities for producing three-dimensional underwater television pictures, very advanced 'deep-down' cinema and still-film photography, and a system for magnetic grappling and seabed exploration.

The full capabilities of this vessel remain secret, but with nonclassified, commercially available sonar able to define at a distance of almost 100 yards a bottom object less than 2 feet square, the exploratory powers of *Mizar* must exceed all previous design limits.

Sonar is the less well publicized cousin of radar. Developed to a great extent during World War II as an anti-submarine detection device, it has undergone dramatic improvements in recent years. Radar and sonar work on the same principle. Wavelengths of different frequencies are generated, then radiated through the air for radar, or water for sonar. When the waves hit something, they are reflected back to the emitting source, and this 'echo' is electronically interpreted by some kind of audio or visual display which supplies the operator with information. Radar uses very-high-frequency radio waves which travel with the speed of light through the atmosphere. Sonar, on the other hand, depends on the much broader wavelengths of sound and these move far more slowly through the denser medium of water.

Recent developments in the deployment of various arrays of sonar signal generators and receivers make it possible, using a combination of side-scanning and bottom-scanning sonar, to produce three-dimensional reports of undersea objects. Another three-dimensional trick in *Mizar*'s bag is a newer and even more remarkable technique called acoustical holography. In this process, sound waves are substituted for the light waves normally used in holography, and a television camera reconstitutes the reflected sound with the aid of a laser beam to produce a holograph, or three-dimensional picture. The pictorial resolution of this technique, at extreme depths where there is absolute darkness, is amazing. Clear, easily readable, tridimensional presentations are displayed on a TV-type screen as the scanning proceeds, providing a continuous view of bottom detail – including sunken wrecks.

Mizar was no stranger to sites of sunken subs, as she had been used as one of the major exploratory tools in the investigation of the causes behind the loss of *USS Thresher*, sunk in 1963 in about 8,000 feet of water, and the later *Scorpion* disaster in '68 which left the boat on the bottom, some 12,000 to 14,000 feet deep. On both occasions, *Mizar* made intensive site surveys, and the crew undoubtedly developed and perfected techniques for this special type of study.

The word 'Mizar' is interesting in itself. It is taken from

the Arabic name of one of the stars in the handle of the Big Dipper. For generations, in the clear skies of the desert, Mizar, a double with a second star, Alcor, has been visible without optical assistance to anyone with 20-20 or better vision. It was used as an eye test by the nomadic tribes. Failure to see the 'rider,' a rough translation of the word 'Alcor', on the back of the horse 'Mizar' was a clear indication of below-normal distance vision. It seems fitting the U.S. Navy's *Mizar* gives us normal vision in ocean depths where no sunlight has ever penetrated, and where even the fish provide their own luminescence.

The ship arrived in the selected area late in June and began a survey to determine what lay on the bottom. The results of this study have never been made public, but experienced scientists conjecture, basing their evaluations on studies of other sites of lost subs, that the Navy found the broken remains of the vessel, surrounded by a ring of metallic debris extending some distance from the main parts of the boat. The debris ring was created by breakage during the fall of the vessel and by material thrown clear by the impact.

Major portions of the stricken ship were lying at an angle of about 33 degrees to the sea floor.

This is more or less the basic pattern found at the sites of both *Scorpion* and *Thresher,* as well as the 'November'-class nuclear Soviet sub lost off Portugal in April 1970. *Thresher,* however, seems to have broken into an unusual number of smaller pieces, and scattered a ring of debris for more than half a mile from a central point. Some specialists conclude this was caused by a series of explosions that may have occurred while the boat was sinking.

None of these facts is consistent with CIA reports that the lost 'Golf'-class boat was found in one piece. It is obvious a complete investigation will have to be made if the truth is to be determined. In the meantime, let Captain Walker's statement suffice. When asked about the apparent raising of the submarine in one piece, *Science* magazine quotes Walker as saying, 'That was quite remarkable to me, considering our experience with *Thresher* and *Scorpion*. I would have expected at least the bow and stern sections to have been fractured off.'

Mizar remained on station for several weeks, operating in strict secrecy and making every effort to avoid contact or notice. The most sophisticated electronic and photographic techniques, combined with systematic magnetic grappling and field readings of the bottom, produced exact information on the position and condition of the sunken vessel. Once the location and site plan had been determined, new space-age technology was brought into play to pinpoint the exact spots where the major components lay, thus allowing for the later establishment of a precise surface position directly above each broken piece. By using computers and the Transit series satellites, a highly accurate fix was obtained.

The Transit instrument packages are a part of the navigational satellite programme NAVSAT. First operational in 1960, this system was designed to provide pinpoint locations for our ICBM missile-carrying submarines, as well as other Navy warships. Extremely exact position plotting is required for accurate missile firing. If you don't know precisely where you are at the time you shoot, you don't really have too much hope of hitting a target thousands of miles away.

Since the original launch of Transit 1B by the Navy, additional vehicles have been orbited. There is now a series of satellites in near-polar orbits at altitudes of about 600 miles.

Once every 12 hours, tracking stations here on earth calculate the latest orbital information for each of the packages, and each satellite stores this in an on-board computer memory. They then transmit this orbit data as they travel through space, sending out a sequence every 120 seconds.

On board ship, the navigator, using the Doppler effect,

determines when the satellite is directly overhead. He feeds the transmitted information, along with the ship speed and the time of the signal receipt, into a specially programmed computer which gives him a precision position fix by numerical printout. The Doppler effect is the name given to a peculiarity of sound waves. As an object, say a locomotive, moves toward an observer, it seems to be making more noise than when it is moving away.

One of the first uses of NAVSAT was to guide the aircraft carrier *Hornet* to the exact splashdown point of the *Yankee Clipper* space module during Pete Conrad's Apollo 12 flight. That feat was all the more remarkable considering the fully overcast sky and the roughness of the sea; either of these two conditions would have made conventional navigation techniques useless. NAVSAT capabilities are now available, commercially, to private users.

From the NAVSAT information, a ship equipped with the proper communications equipment and an on-board computer capability could precisely locate a spot in the middle of the largest ocean on earth and take station within inches of the *Mizar*-plotted resting place of each part of the lost submarine.

Along with navigational data, *Mizar* also developed pictures of outstanding resolution, showing the condition of the wreckage. According to informed sources, these electronic photos revealed a major difference between the sunken vessel and some of her sister 'Golf'-class boats. This sub had undergone the changes mentioned earlier, and the sail, or what was once called the conning tower, of the shattered wreck had been modified to house three of the more advanced, 700-mile-range, full-megaton nuclear-warhead Serb-class missiles. Whether missiles were actually on board was a question, although certainly tests were run to attempt to detect their presence. The proof of the capability of this class boat to carry longer-range, more effective atomic weapons was of major interest to those involved with the project and of vital importance in determining U.S. evaluations of future Strategic Arms Limitation Treaty (SALT) talks.

Mizar remained on station for almost two months, sweeping the area, and by late August had accomplished its mission. The information it developed, forwarded to the highest echelons of the Navy, provided a complete picture of the site, the sunken ship and the difficulties involved in recovery.

Mizar has been active in several other sea-floor studies since her visit to the Jennifer site, and an unofficial spokesman in the Underseas Systems Branch of the Navy revealed privately in May 1976 she would shortly commence an evaluation of the sea floor of the Indian Ocean, in an effort to determine why 'the Indian Ocean is a vast question mark on how acoustics work.' Apparently, due to special conditions existing on the bottom of this area, sonar readings are, at times, questionable. The reasons for this are obscure, but are of vital importance not only for understanding undersea geology, but also for developing reliable, worldwide antisubmarine warfare capabilities. A mission of major magnitude is apparently planned to seek out the anomalies beneath this particular body of water, identify them and devise means of surmounting them.

By September 1968, the Navy was in possession of a massive amount of information about the sunken submarine. *Mizar* had not been ordered to the site to satisfy idle curiosity. Somewhere, in someone's mind, the idea of a possible retrieval had formed, and at least a part of the survey effort had been to estimate the value of the intelligence we would gain if our side could actually raise the vessel and salvage its contents.

3

The concept of recovering another nation's 'lost' military equipment was not a new one. But the audacity of giving serious thought to an operation requiring bottom grappling at depths of over three miles caused serious concern in the upper echelons of the Navy. There was interest at the highest levels, but also, naturally, hesitance. Such a programme would cost millions of dollars. To develop support for the project, a major study would be required to evaluate the techniques available to make the pickup and the probable return on the investment. An analysis of this nature, including an itemization of the specific information to be gained, would require long hours of work by a diverse group of specialists.

The exact evolution of the operation through the chain of command is impossible to follow; even the names of the naval hierarchy in favour of the programme have never been released. But it is clear from published reports little time was wasted in bringing the matter before the then Deputy Secretary of Defense David Packard. And in Packard, the project found a practical, understanding reception.

Fifty-six-year-old David Packard, a big, 6-foot 4-inch, 250-pound outdoorsman, was a self-made millionaire-industrialist from California. Co-founder, along with

William R. Hewlett, of the huge Hewlett-Packard Company, a major manufacturer of a multitude of electronics products for science and industry, he brought to his Defense Department job a strong and able administrative capability including a finely honed sense of how to manage people.

He was also technically trained, having received a degree in electronics from Stanford University. While in college, Packard distinguished himself socially as president of his fraternity, athletically in football and basketball, and academically by being named to both Phi Beta Kappa and Sigma Xi.

Known to his colleagues as a contemporary man, he entered into his government office as a proven, top-flight administrator and a good balance to the Secretary of Defense, Melvin Laird.

According to published accounts, Packard became interested in the Jennifer Project and directed an investigation be made to outline the intelligence possibilities which might be derived from the recovery of the wreckage. This is the point at which Operation Jennifer begins to take shape, because the report delivered to Packard is said to have included the recommendation for a recovery effort.

No official comment has been made on how long it took the special panel of intelligence experts, scientists, engineers and technicians to work through the gathered data and produce a programme, but it was a short time. By November, things had progressed to the point of considering the machinery required for the pickup, and a California firm, Mechanics Research, Inc., was employed for an evaluation.

An impressive list of potential intelligence information was compiled and must have included all the following:

First, there was the possiblity of the recovery of one or more Serb-class missiles, and the equipment used in the SS-N-5 launching system. This alone would be worth a

35

phenomenal price, because at that time, we knew very little about the Soviet state of nuclear and missile art.

A group of creative engineers armed with a small part of a total system can develop a remarkably accurate view of the whole system. As an example, in 1944 during World War II, a team of British intelligence experts turned over to a group of aeronautical engineers a small piece of wing section from a destroyed V-1 'Buzz Bomb' rocket. The section was less than a foot and a half square. Working around the clock and using various testing facilities available to them, the engineering team delivered a report in a matter of days. They described the entire rocket in great detail, producing a possible working drawing and were even able to cite its range and warhead weight.

After the war, when German documents fell into British hands, the description was checked and found to be generally correct even as to some side speculations the engineers had made about the accuracy of the pulse-jet-powered missile.

All things considered, such reconstruction capability is not really too surprising. At any given time, the state of the art in a given technology is known to a number of people who deal with the principles involved in that technology on a daily basis. Given a portion of an unknown unit, accurate deduction of the whole is a matter of working from known capabilities and applying them back to the sample fragment or component.

Thus, recovery of an unfired missile would provide a fantastic array of worthwhile facts and facilitate counter-measure design. Acquisition of the firing system would also be invaluable.

A second area of interest must have been the nuclear-tipped torpedoes 'Golf'-class subs were known to carry. According to published sources, an unknown complement of such torpedoes was included in the standard fleet arsenal of boats of this type. In the early 60's, this class of vessel was estimated to carry up to 40 'fish' but no report was available for their capacity after modification.

To gain an actual nuclear warhead and see the Soviet level of atomic sophistication firsthand would be priceless from the standpoint of future technical development.

And the possibility of determining the homing devices incorporated into the design of the torpedo would offer an irresistible challenge to those entrusted with the programming of naval countermeasures designed to make the 'fish' miss its intended target.

So there was enough potential information on the atomic side of the ledger alone to make the trip worthwhile. There was also a great deal more.

Many published reports have mentioned the possibility of acquiring the sunken submarine's code books or code machine. In all probability, the Russians would have changed their codes as soon as the ship was known to be missing. But U.S. files contain hundreds of intercepted messages on magnetic tape, and possibly these could be deciphered. A basic understanding of the philosophy and technique behind the development of the Soviet code system would be a landmark acquisition for designing computer programmes to attempt to decode future guarded messages. Further, a code machine is a complex electronic device, and if a Soviet one could be studied to determine its design logic, this would facilitate future code-breaking efforts.

As interesting as the codes were, the possiblity of getting a firsthand look at the Ship's Internal Guidance System (SIGS) or the Ship's Internal Navigation System (SINS) was even more exciting. Either of these units could provide technicians with the ability to predict the accuracy of a Soviet vessel's navigation, which vitally affects the accuracy of a launched missile.

Both the SIGS and SINS are complicated, space-age products. Without them any thought of accurate nuclear missile firing from submarines would be pure fantasy. The ability to constantly check and recheck the exact

37

position of the sub, even through days of deep submergence, is necessary if any real expectation is held of directing a missile to its target. If you don't know exactly where you are, you have no way to point the missile during launch or to direct it in flight. Thus some form of SINS device is absolutely vital, and a look at one from another country would provide us with estimates of the accuracy of their missiles at a given range.

The radio gear on board would also reveal several interesting things, including the ability of the Soviet submarine fleet to send and receive messages without surfacing some form of antenna. In our own Navy, this is a top-secret area, but special ultra-low-frequency radio communications can be maintained with any of our sophisticated nuclear subs even when they are deeply submerged under a polar icecap.

Another useful find would be the metal of the ship itself and a section of welded joint. Working from only a bit or a piece, a company of experts could deduce the operating depth and speeds of the vessel, gain a base for judging future designs and steel qualities, get some idea of production times required and the level of sophistication of Soviet erecting yards. The welds themselves would reveal the state of their technology.

Part numbers stamped onto various components would clearly show the place of manufacture. Even materials in short supply might be indicated by substitutions, for example, of fibre for neoprene rubber in gaskets or of aluminium for copper in large wiring hookups. The state of Soviet knowledge about our antisubmarine warfare techniques could also be judged by studying their countermeasure systems.

Finally, additional data could be obtained from any remaining letters, messages, maps, radio-frequency books, operating manuals and other run-of-the-mill items carried as standard on a commissioned vessel performing a mission on the high seas. The list of intelligence material available for the taking was impressive.

And when we add the natural desire of the professionals in the spy business to carry out a major field operation, and the amount of innovative daring and intrigue required in a project of this magnitude, we can suppose a most favourable report was made on the project.

4

One problem which faced the appointed group of experts was the question of how, if it proved desirable, could the task of recovering the sunken sub be achieved? To understand how this question was answered, we need to return to the year 1957.

Dwight Eisenhower, the military hero of the European Theatre of Operations in World War II, was completing his first term as our country's 34th President; the Common Market was formed in Europe, marking the start of a new cooperation among the countries of that rebuilding continent, and Milwaukee took the World's Series from New York, four games to three, in a tight playoff.

In a spirit of cooperation, scientists and engineers from about 70 nations, along with their governments, banded together, pooling funds, for an eighteen-month period called the International Geophysical Year (IGY). Its purpose was to devote the best minds available to the study of the earth, the oceans, the atmosphere and the sun, in an effort to solve many of the questions which have perplexed man since the dawn of time. Many research installations, several still in use today, were constructed during this period.

The IGY is remarkable and memorable because of two

major projects. The dominant event was the Soviet launching of the first artificial satellite. On October 4, 1957, Sputnik 1 successfully orbited the earth, and its blast-off was the starter's gun in the race to the moon.

The other project recieved a great deal of publicity in late '57 and early '58 but, unlike Sputnik, achieved no immediately significant results. Its long-term attainments, however, were to prove very dramatic indeed.

The geologically inclined contingent of the IGY heard and adopted a proposal to explore not only outward, but inward, as well. The earth as a planet is covered with a thick outer layer called the crust. All known life takes place on this surface. While there are many theories about the makeup of the interior of the earth, even our deepest oil wells have not come close to penetrating this outer layer and actually sampling the fringe of the Mohorovicic discontinuity (or Moho) which is the dividing layer between the outer crust and the earth's core.

It was a stated goal of the IGY to conduct Project Mohole, the drilling of a hole for sampling purposes into the Moho. To do this required a major planning effort to select a site where the earth's outer layer was thin enough for the then-available technology to penetrate with a drill string. The spot proved to be on the bottom of the ocean, where, according to experts, the crust was at its thinnest.

The problem became, then, not the development of a better or more effective deep drilling system, but the conception of a very stable, fixed-position, floating drill platform.

Deep-hole drilling, such as is used in oil exploration, is accomplished by using sections of thick-wall metal tubing, called drill pipe. These are threaded, one at a time, onto a drill bit which makes the actual hole through the earth. The pipe sections, available in various lengths, are rotated, causing the bit to operate and 'make hole', as they say on the drilling rigs. As the bit goes deeper, the pipe string follows it and, one at a time, additional lengths of drill pipe are added to the string of pipe operating down in the hole.

Steel pipe, while strong, is not very flexible. Imagine what would happen in an attempt to drill from a normal ship. The drill string would be lowered to the sea floor, and would start making hole. Pipe would be added, a length at a time, and the drill would pass rapidly through the softness of the first few hundred feet. Everything would be fine until the first wave moved the ship more than a few yards from its original position. Then, all hell would break loose.

The drill string, anchored on the bottom, hundreds of feet deep in mud, would be subjected to enormous bending forces. When it finally passed its design strengths, it would snap, releasing tons of kinetic energy. A close parallel would be a stretched cable on a winch breaking under tension. Few things are more dangerous than severed cable ends whipping through the air with deadly force, striking out like twisting steel snakes.

There is a second major problem with seabed drilling. The same wave or swell which moves the ship away from its station also 'heaves' the ship upward, then lowers it. Drill pipe, which can take stress in tension, or stretch, cannot tolerate equally high compression forces, and when the ship moves down off the swell, which can easily be a distance of ten to twelve feet, the string would actually be supporting the multi-ton vessel like a thin steel column.

In short, some serious problems were associated with the Mohole plan. But even in 1957, the difficulties in holding an exact station over a drill site and compensating the drilling platform and drill string for the most damaging effects of sea motion were considered to be more easily solvable than the problems which would be encountered in ultra-deep-hole dry-land drilling.

One man was an early leader in the development of deep-sea drilling techniques.

Willard N. Bascom, described by one scientific journal as an 'engineer of genius but no degree,' was vitally interested in the Mohole effort and was a key member of the concept and design staff. When funds for the project failed to materialize, Bascom, along with a select group of associates, left Mohole to found a progressive company called Ocean Science and Engineering, Inc. OSE approached the CIA in the early 1960's with a plan to use a stationary ship, equipped with a stable derrick platform which compensated for swell action, to lower a claw-type grapple on a string of specially constructed pipes and recover missile nose cones off Palmyra, one of the Line Islands in the Pacific. A subsequent proposal was made in late 1963, after the sinking of *USS Thresher*, to recover all or part of the vessel.

The CIA apparently rejected both proposals, but Bascom's ideas clearly set the stage for the Jennifer Project, and when the need arose, there was, in all likelihood, a dossier on Bascom's and OSE's suggestions and methods.

Bascom's techniques were no theoretical hodgepodge. In addition to being granted U.S. Patent No. 3,215,976, for a deep-sea search and recovery system, he designed a special vessel for using it, the *Alcoa Seaprobe*, which was constructed by the Alcoa Marine Corporation in 1971.

Years later, after portions of the story of the Jennifer Project became public, Bascom, through his attorney, George Wise of Long Beach, California, would question whether his patent rights had been infringed. A spokesman for Global Marine, Taylor Hancock, an officer of the firm assigned to design and supervise the construction of the *Hughes Glomar Explorer,* said the technology they used was 'vastly different' from Bascom's concepts. And although he declined to describe those differences, a review of the techniques seems to bear out Hancock's claim.

Even so, since at least 1971, the CIA had in its files an

outline of a possible way of making the deep seabed recovery of an object.

To study the matter, the U.S. Government entered into a top-secret agreement with a small Californian firm called Mechanics Research, Inc. (MRI). The preliminary work by MRI related to certain improvements in the state of the art, but their abilities, by all indications, were limited to a theoretical level. The time had come for a more practical look at the possible recovery methods.

Global Marine, Inc., a company noted for its technical excellence in undersea engineering, was a logical choice to perform the evaluation and critique of the work already in progress. In January and February 1970, a contract was arranged by the CIA, between Global Marine, Inc. and MRI, for this purpose. Global Marine had several operating oil drilling rigs mounted on ships, and its personnel was familiar with the available technology in the field of petroleum exploration.

The team assembled under the direction of R. Curtis Crooke, John Evans and John Graham found new and unusual difficulties. The problems of making a down-deep pickup were different and more demanding than those for simple drilling. The need for more precise station-keeping, some form of compensation for the heave of the vessel, and isolation of the working platform from the roll and pitch of the ship are all a part of trying to lift a heavy weight from a great depth. But the problems were fully understood and appreciated. And some thinking had gone into solutions.

The elements needed to make up a successful operation were coming together.

First, there was the motive, the reason for the project in the first place. The great amount of technical information to be gained by a successful raising of the submarine made the attempt more than worthwhile; and, in fact, made it almost mandatory to try.

Second, there were a number of influential individuals

willing to involve themselves in an undertaking of this magnitude. And even in the planning stages, the project must have seemed huge. A special ship, with no existing counterpart, had to be designed and built. Then a crew had to be trained to handle the sophisticated equipment on board as well as to care for themselves on a dangerous mission in international waters. The crew also had to be skilled in the problems of radiation contamination, in case any of the nuclear warheads had 'leaked' from the abnormal stresses placed on them. All this had to be done while maintaining absolute secrecy.

Assuming all the above could be accomplished clandestinely, a specialized ship had to be taken to a site in the middle of the Pacific Ocean without attracting undue attention. Once there, it had to probe at depths never before attempted for the remnants of the broken sub. And if they were successful, they had to somehow bring back the recovered items, and still maintain the secret nature of the entire undertaking.

The third ingredient was the technology and skill to make the plan practical. The CIA had some access to basic techniques, but making them work would be a difficult task, even for a country with the scientific, technical and manufacturing capabilities of the United States.

One final thing was lacking – the money to pay for it all. And it was apparent from the first, this project was going to take a bunch of bucks.

5

Undoubtedly, the intelligence analysis returned to David Packard clearly indicated the value of the proposed recovery operation and outlined the many benefits accruing from a successful completion of the mission. Packard, who was new to his Defense Department office, having taken his oath in January 1969, was impressed with the prospects for success, so he lent support to the undertaking.

Up to this point, although experts had been called in from other governmental offices, the entire operation had been under control of the Navy. But the scope of the programme and the need for secrecy officially brought in the Central Intelligence Agency, which began its own private evaluation of the chances of the project's success. Its findings must have agreed with those of the report sent to Packard.

While the Navy and the CIA had their differences concerning the operation, some accord must have been reached by the top echelons because the two agencies ultimately cooperated in the venture.

An interesting quote appeared in *Time*, in March 1975. An unnamed deputy director of the CIA was reportedly assigned the job of presenting the programme to the then CIA Director Richard Helms. 'He damn near threw me out the window,' said the deputy, recalling Helms' reaction. ' "You must be crazy," he told me.'

Obviously, at some point, Helms' startled initial reaction changed, because CIA involvement began in earnest and a virtual parade of high-ranking naval officers began to pass through the Langley, Virginia, complex.

Another source indicates Helms became personally active in the project. This would be very much in keeping with one of the basic motivations for CIA enthusiasm in the first place. In addition to gaining fabulous amounts of information for research and development programmes and one-upping the Russians, it was sort of like old times. It made the spy business fun again.

A problem with grave international overtones now arose, and proposed a serious threat to the entire operation. And this same problem, in a slightly different form, has been one of the main factors in the United States Government's official silence on the Jennifer Project.

Since the end of the International Geophysical Year, an important controversy had been brewing over the various nations' right to the ocean floor. The seabed, outside the boundaries claimed by countries as their continental limits, is international, and as such is governed by a large body of agreements and treaties composing the Law of the Sea.

These regulations, which control what may or may not be done in or under international waters, cannot be taken lightly. Since the middle 1950's, the so-called developing or third-world nations have taken a highly vociferous and adamant stand on matters affecting the seabed. They have repeatedly argued for the immediate creation of an international regime with absolute control over all operations conducted on the sea floor outside continental limits.

The 'group of 77' developing nations has pressed its stand both to our government and to the United Nations. And they have generated sufficient support for their plans

47

to make them useful as a pressure point in international relations.

The Soviets, when faced with their demands, respond as they always do. If it temporarily suits their purpose, they acquiesce – in a fashion designed to make the United States appear to be the main source of blockage. On other occasions, when it is more in their interests to disagree, they simply remain silent, ignoring everything.

The U.S. is in an especially vulnerable position on the question of international control over the sea floor, because we are almost the only ones who have the present capability to perform practical tasks there. Several privately owned mining interest groups are ready to begin long-term projects for the recovery of minerals from this hostile environment.

So the entire question of international law governing the seabed made Jennifer a diplomatic hot potato. The State Department's attorneys almost immediately came to grips with the Navy's legal staff, which was itself divided. While one group of top brass was promoting the programme in every possible way, another group of naval attorneys was arguing the illegality of the act of recovering or salvaging a Soviet vessel in international waters.

The lawyers from the State Department countered not with a legal difference of opinion, but with fact. The Soviets themselves had on specific occasions salvaged the vessels of other nations, and by so doing exhibited a complete disregard for the fine points of the law. Their acquisition of Nazi U-boats at the end of World War II is an excellent example. But the question remained tricky.

It is known the CIA sided with the State Department attorneys, but the best thing CIA Director Colby could muster to say on the subject later was the project 'always operated on the fringes.'

After disposing of the Navy's opposing argument, State's attorneys persisted in pointing to the controlling importance of existing agreements concerning the inter-

48

national nature of the seabed. This position was, of course, entirely consistent with both U.S. policy statements and position reports from most of the concerned branches of government.

While this legal storm was brewing, Packard, satisfied with the potential for success of the activity and convinced of the enormous return on the projected investment, gave his OK to the programme and authorized its submission to the 40 Committee.

The 40 Committee, so called because it was established in 1948 by memo No. 40 under Harry Truman's Presidency as an offshoot of the National Security Act of 1947, was the final review group for approving all intelligence actions. It also oversaw the general activity of the CIA. At this time, the group was composed of five key people, including one or more representatives from the Department of Defense, the State Department, the Director of the CIA, and the Chairman of the Joint Chiefs of Staff.

This group began an examination of the projected Jennifer Project, and ran smack into the still unresolved legal questions. The 40 Committee was charged to evaluate the overall impact of each intelligence operation. Necessarily, it had to contemplate the negative reactions of a programme which failed or, worse, was 'broken' and became public knowledge. The members were obliged to take serious account both of the legal hassle between the Navy and the Department of State and of the pressures from the third-world countries for an internationally controlled sea floor.

The third-world attitudes were of particular importance, because U.S. relations with these nations appeared to be worsening. We had been actively attacked in the U.N., were involved in a very unpopular position on South Asia and were facing Soviet alignment with many of the smaller African nations.

Another problem, smaller in scope, but equally explosive as far as the individuals on the committee were concerned, was the relative roles of the CIA and the Navy.

The Navy, after all, had instigated the whole affair. They had turned to the CIA for assistance, and now the CIA was emerging as the prime controlling force, moving the Navy into a subservient role. Apparently the Navy's desire for the information to be retrieved finally overcame its distaste at being made to occupy a back seat, and it continued to support the programme financially as well as emotionally. But the already existing divisions among the top naval commanders concerning the value of the project were intensifying as the result of growing concern about the propriety of CIA leadership and the competence of its director.

During the in-fighting, the question arose of the CIA's right to conduct a mission such as this, and it lingered until a National Security Council (NSC) ruling, the very secret 10-2, was invoked. The 10-2, passed by the NSC in 1948, stated the CIA could undertake 'special operations, always provided they were secret, and sufficiently diminutive in size as to be plausibly denied by the government.'

One of the interesting insights to come from all this behind-the-scenes manoeuvring is the very orderly fashion in which things are accomplished. Precedent is important. As are specific acts or laws allowing or disallowing certain courses of action by a governed body. While it is clear each individual on the committee had his personal point of view, and acted, where possible, to forward his position, all were aware of being controlled by the structure of the government they were serving.

No public record exists indicating how long the 40 Committee cussed and discussed the various aspects of the operation. The heaviest debate must have concerned the problems arising in international relations if the somewhat aggressive act ever came to light. The third-world countries, surely backed by the U.S.S.R., would create serious international tensions. Yet a deciding issue must have been the desirability of establishing a precedent for deep-sea recovery in international waters. Armed with the accomplished fact, negotiators, in years to come, would be possessed of a card which they could play or not at their discretion.

In fact, the authorization for the Jennifer Project set the rule allowing for the later 1970 U.S. recovery of a nuclear weapon from a Soviet aircraft which crashed in the Sea of Japan, a U.S. Navy recovery of electronic eavesdropping equipment from a sunken trawler in '71, and a joint U.S.-British salvage operation of electronic gear from a crashed Soviet plane in the North Sea in '72.

After numerous meetings, outside committee reports and long debates, the operation received a somewhat hesitant approval. The 40 Committee, after voting its agreement, passed the arguments, plans and recommendations, as was required, to the President for his personal and final OK. Richard Nixon, acting in his role as Commander-in-Chief, gave the final authorization, and Jennifer became a reality.

Several members of Congress also knew about the plan. Senator Milton Young of North Dakota, then the ranking Republican on the Defense Appropriations Committee, which handles most of the CIA's financing, reportedly recalls Democratic Senator John McClellan of Arkansas and the late Senators Richard Russell and Allen Ellender were informed of the operation and briefed on its particulars.

The entire matter of Congressional knowledge of top-secret operations is a very touchy subject. On the one hand, Congress, through its subcommittees, is charged with the responsibility of overseeing and controlling to some degree the activities of the armed services and all governmental agencies.

But how many people can keep a secret? How many individuals really have a need to know? Or, at least, to know everything? The very nature of intelligence work requires secrecy, and secrecy cannot be maintained if large numbers of people who are exercising control are each told the full details of a project.

Members of the Intelligence Subcommittee of the Senate Armed Services Committee are faced with a difficult task. They must learn enough about a project or operation to form some opinion as to its merits, but not so much as to inadvertently jeopardize the action. And, since the committee acts as a whole, every member must be equally well informed. The problems inherent in Congressional control of intelligence activities are monumental, and a solution needs to be developed. Suffice it to say, in the case of the Jennifer Project, Congressional briefing probably did not extend as far as it could have.

Jennifer was now a reality. All approval was granted. The only thing missing was the actual funding.

Where the money came from and how much was needed are still mysteries and have been the subjects of a number of errors in reporting. The Navy was deeply interested and had research and development funding it could use. The CIA was not without resources and could produce additional allotments for special operations, as required. Undoubtedly, a combination of these two sources, with the probable addition of others, was used.

Pacific Ocean, a maritime magazine, reports almost a half billion dollars was diverted by the CIA from allotments to naval research. And the March 1976 issue of *Sea Technology* a publication devoted to maritime design, said, 'An attempt to raise a Russian "Golf" class submarine in the Pacific, northwest of Hawaii, was financed by the U.S. Navy under orders from higher echelon despite official opposition.' What 'official opposition' to Project Jennifer there was in the Navy was not indicated and it seems, in the face of the facts, to be a rather strong statement.

Likewise, $500,000,000 is an enormous amount of money, and few other published reports indicate an expenditure of anywhere near that amount. Recent research has produced evidence of a lower cost for the programme.

In private conversations with government officials, who have asked not to be named, the question of the cost of the hardware and operations for the Jennifer Project was considered. These officials, who have access to many of the actual financial records and to subsequent evaluations of the ship built for the operation, declined to name a figure. When sources were quoted to them indicating the cost of the programme was in excess of $400 million, however, they showed their disbelief in the high figure. They did concede a total budget for the operation of about $130 million would be 'right about on the money'. A breakdown of the expenditures makes this figure believable.

The required ship was to cost about $30 million, but overruns brought the price up to $40 million. Another $40 million was required to construct a special service barge and other equipment. Additional funds, estimated to be about $10 million to $12 million, were used for the pipe string and lift system. Another $10 million was needed for a series of mobile laboratories for use in analysing recovered items. Thus about $100 million went for what can be more or less called hardware. The balance, about another $30 million, was for operational expenses and crew training.

Even allowing for some conservatism on the part of the officials, a total of $200 million would seem more than adequate for the accomplishment of the job at hand. And $200 million is about the amount quoted when stories of the project first appeared.

In summary, the motive was clear. The inclination to act was present. The plan and technology were available. Funding had been approved throughout the chain of command. It was time to turn the paper tiger into a real-life, fire-breathing monster. Project Jennifer was finally operational.

6

The CIA was now confronted with a task of almost unmanageable proportions.

For starters, they had to complete the research being performed in their labs to determine the amounts of damage various types of paper and ink would receive from sustained soaking in pressurized sea water. This same series of experiments also would indicate the best possible treatment to give such documents to restore them. NASA was brought in for part of this through use of one of their huge space research vacuum chambers. Since water will boil and vaporize at very low temperatures when air pressure is low, even the wettest paper can be dried by 'boiling away' the water with very little heat in near-vacuum conditions.

This same sequence of experiments also indicated the best ways to salvage plastics and printed circuits, as well as nuclear devices which might, due to the immense pressures upon them, prove to leak. The culmination of this portion of the project coincided with the master planning stage, and the various technical problems were discussed and solved in detail.

Global Marine had submitted, in August 1970, a four-volume proposal for the design and construction of the complete system necessary to perform the task. This report became a part of the final presentations to gain approval of the project.

With money in hand, the CIA negotiated a final agreement between Global Marine, Hughes Tool Company (soon to become Summa Corporation) and the U.S. Government. This contract, revised and finalized in December 1972, was numbered S-Hu-0900. It named Global Marine as Systems Engineering Technical Director (S.E.T.D.) for the project and allowed it to start actual planning for the design of the vessel.

By late August, the original ideas were fully accepted by the U.S. Government, and Global Marine let contracts with such diverse companies as FAG Bearings (a German concern), Minneapolis Honeywell, General Motors, Western Gear, Nordberg Engines, General Electric, Cooper-Bessemer and others.

The original Global Marine presentation called for the development of a complete system, including several major fabrications. To begin with, they would need a ship, but not just any ship. They had to contract for the construction of a vessel unique in the annals of marine design and then follow it through every phase, from laying the first steel to sea trials, solving unanticipated technical difficulties.

A visit to the *Hughes Glomar Explorer* indicates the level of the problem. It is one of the most advanced-concept vessels ever created, and the ship itself is a technical achievement equal to the Mercury and Apollo series space capsules.

The first impression of the vessel is one of immense size. At 618 feet 8 inches, it is longer than two football fields, and its height to the top of the main derrick is 263 feet, or about the same as a 23-storey building.

But once on board, the impression of sheer size dwindles, and the complexity of overall design grows as each new facet of the vessel is revealed. Everything necessary for a complement of up to 178 people has been carefully thought out, including an extensive health-care centre with the latest surgical and medical equipment.

Before the vessel could be constructed, there were several specific projects requiring engineering attention. The station-keeping system had to be perfected. It was imperative for the ship to be able to hold its position on the recovery site to within feet of the precisely selected spot. Then a special 'heavy lift' system was needed to raise the enormous tonnage of the sunken sub. The built-in heave and roll motion compensators were a vital part of the ship's construction plans.

Next there was the question of how to grapple onto the submarine. A great claw had to be designed and built. The monstrous control device, called the strongback, had to be made in one piece for utmost strength. The strong-back would form the backbone of the grappling system, and in addition to controlling the actions of the claw, it would be able to be made buoyant by the addition of surface air. This buoyancy would serve to lighten the total weight to be lifted.

The claw and strongback presented another problem. Together they would weigh in at well over 6 million pounds. To say they were big is an understatement of some magnitude. They were huge. Unless the ship could be literally built around them, there was no way to lift such objects and swing them on board. The A-frame and derrick structure of the lifting system would prevent this.

A whole plan had to be concocted for the hookup of the grapple to the pipe string. This would involve using a huge submersible barge with a steel roof to keep its cargo covered from aerial surveillance.

Other things were required as well. The laboratory boys, who would be responsible for examining the salvaged pieces of the wreck, developed list after list of possible tests they might be called upon to run, and other lists of equipment they would need. There was no way all this could be constructed inside the vessel, so a series of trailers or vans was ordered, borrowed or commandeered. Some were already fitted out to be laboratories for different scientific disciplines. Others were custom-made to perform tasks not usually required.

Personnel was also an immediate consideration. People were needed to do everything from welding to clothes-washing, from cleaning toilet bowls to decontaminating a hot nuclear device without exploding it.

To some extent, Carl Duckett was involved in most of these problems and decisions. Since he was Deputy Director of the CIA in charge of the Directorate of Science and Technology, most of this work flowed through his section.

There was a deep controversy through the years 1970 and 1971 over the growing complexity of the undertaking. It is one thing to sit in a room and view slides with backup diagrams and agree such a mission is possible; it's another to try to make the picture-book symbol for a ship into reality. Arguments over Jennifer during 1970 and into 1971 inside the Nixon Administration were a common occurrence. Technical failures, cost overruns and the ever-present fear of detection and the effect knowledge of the project would have on a shaky detente were all subjects of hot debate.

No one is certain how close the project came to being closed down, or upon how many occasions the people involved suffered criticism for the growing complexities. The pressures must have been intense. Finally, in 1971, the contracts for the construction of the hardware were let.

A small, but significant number of technical experts had kept things alive. They were driven, in part, by recollections about some Soviet armament captured in the '67 Israeli-Arab war during the Johnson Administration. Enormous amounts of time had been spent on estimating the effectiveness of these various weapons, but, since the evaluations were made without even so much as a spent cartridge case to use as a basis for deduction, the estimates proved to be far short of reality. Or, as one

White House aide said at the time, 'not very accurate.' Now, with planning under way for the Strategic Arms Limitations Talks (SALT), a sound appraisal of the Soviet sub fleet's strike potential was mandatory.

The major problem which began to emerge as the operation progressed was the number of people involved. From a hundred or so, in the first stages, to thousands from every level of life and diverse professions and occupations. By the time the basic planning was done, probably more than 500 individuals had direct, specific knowledge of the mission.

Then drawings had to be made, and crew recruitment started. Suddenly there were more than 1,000 people with information. Then the construction of the ship and barge began. Not to mention the pipe, the ancillary lift equipment, the claw and the strongback.

By the time of the ship's completion, with crew training and operations manuals written, proficiency tests completed, necessary vessel inspections passed, insurance arranged for, electronic navigation equipment installed and approved, and sea tests completed for the various working systems, it was hard to estimate the number of people who had worked with the project or had a very direct contact with someone who was into the action.

An independent study indicates that when the *Hughes Glomar Explorer* took station at the recovery site in the Pacific, more than 4,000 people had been involved in the operation. Many had been screened and given some level of security clearance. Only a few knew the entire story, but since modern espionage is the slow piecing together of an innumerable number of bits into a complete, mosaic whole, Project Jennifer was as vulnerable to penetration and exposure as any operation since the Manhattan Project, which started with a few specialists in the early 1940's during World War II and grew to employ over 5,000 people.

The press and other information-gathering agencies became more aggressive in their search for information.

Seymour Hersh of *The New York Times*, for instance, started an investigation of the affair in 1973, but stopped his research at the request of CIA Director Colby.

A successful intelligence operation must be, by definition, secret. No one must learn of it, much less its success or failure. Information is effective only when others don't know you have it. This was especially true of Jennifer.

A confrontation in nonterritorial waters over a U.S. vessel's engagement in the quasi-legal recovery of another nation's ship of war would cause an international incident of a size sufficient to dwarf the one created when Francis Gary Powers, one of our U-2 spy plane pilots, was shot down over Russia while engaged in a top-secret high-altitude reconnaissance mission.

A confrontation on the high seas was unthinkable. Which was probably the reason for Henry Kissinger's lack of enthusiasm for the whole Jennifer affair. As Nixon's national security adviser, he was privy to the details and was either nonsupportive or at least very negative towards the project. Some of his hesitancy must have come from his strong feelings about the policy of detente as an operating philosophy. Public disclosure, which must have seemed to him a likely prospect, not to mention an open ocean face-off with the Russians, would deal his detente programme a very hard blow.

In his position, Kissinger could have stopped Jennifer before it was started, or at least halted it in its still formative stages. But he did not. Which again indicates the value of the information everyone felt could be recovered. It was worth the risk.

But if security were to slip, even a little, trouble was a certainty. And there was no rational way to expect each and every one of the people involved to keep silent. Nor is it easy to hide the construction of a very large ship of peculiar design being built from very unusual plans.

It was plain even in the initial stages an elaborate cover story would have to be developed and released if the mission were to remain covert. The cover would have to take care of a great many different things.

First, there were the ship, the barge and the other hardware. The story would have to provide a sound reason for their construction and, since they could have no connection with the government, this meant there had to be a clearly definable profit or scientific motive.

Then there was the matter of the crew and its training. Many of the workers would need to have had at least a few years of experience in the oil drilling industry, which is a business rife with independent characters and loose talk of drilling tries and finds. The men who make their living on the offshore rigs and platforms are a hardy breed, close knit and open to their own kind. To believe they would not discuss the project with their friends would be foolish. So the same story had to provide cover for the personnel who would work the ship's systems.

Another difficulty was the need for an esoteric array of electronic equipment, including the latest in navigational aids and computer control systems. No ship in service needed the precise pinpointing of its location required for the operation of the *Hughes Glomar Explorer*.

There were additional problems. For example, the individuals who would train the operators of the vessel in one or another of its functions. Unless a secrecy oath were required from each and every one, including those who would write the training manuals, there was always the possibility of disclosure.

Some of the training itself would be impossible to mask. Courses would have to be held in Russian to aid in the disassembly of the recovered artifacts. And precautions on the handling of nuclear or radioactive materials would be a vital part of the curriculum. There was no way to provide cover for these two necessary areas of instruction. So the mission needed a secret air, allowing the crew to be instructed in private.

The cover story had to be a good one. It had to provide

an economic motive for the ship, somehow be secret enough to cause people to keep quiet of their own volition and, finally, be plausible to the press.

Or, better still, the cover should be strong enough to stand on its own and be deliberately leaked. That way, after the initial flurry of public attention, the ship and its mission would fade into a kind of limbo, and the vessel could be utilized for its true purposes.

According to one unnamed source, the idea of a treasure hunt was put forward as accomplishing all the cover goals. Such a hunt for a sunken ship required discretion or everyone and his brother would be on the scene trying to fish up gold and silver. The treasure hunt theme would have had appeal to certain CIA staffers. There are few more glamorous adventures than a full-blown hunt for lost gold on the high seas. Books have been full of this kind of thing for years. Moreover, treasure hunting by trying to recover an entire sunken ship was close enough to the reality of the mission to mask many overt slips.

But a treasure hunt was somehow undignified. Also, it had in it, the nasty potential of causing Congress to look into the misappropriation of funds by the CIA in a cockamamy search for lost treasure.

No, the cover needed to have more legitimacy and be interesting, but not as intriguing to the press as a treasure hunt. There had to be something of the same element of secrecy in it, though, to insure closed mouths to back-up formal security agreements.

It is probable the State Department came up with the best idea. At least they had to approve it.

Ocean research had long ago indicated the presence on the seabed of nodules of solid copper, nickel and other nonferrous metals. Scientists do not agree on the reason for the existence of these almost pure metal ingots, but most opinions indicate they were formed when molten magma erupted from the sea floor and spewed white-hot drops into the chill, deep waters.

The area in which the sub had gone down, according to both published technical articles and the independent study performed by the Navy while on site, was rich in these nodules. A National Science Foundation (NSF) study performed in 1973 concluded the deposits off the Hawaiian plateau were the most abundant in the North Pacific and contained high values of both copper and nickel.

There had been some talk, in scientific circles, of using a kind of bottom scraper to harvest these lumps, and several economic studies had been made to determine the amount of various metals that it would be necessary to recover to make such a project profitable.

The seabed mining story would also account for the need of the ship to be on the site at a particular time. By admitting some form of down-deep bottom prospecting, the weather problem could be openly discussed.

Because of the nature of the waves and swell in the recovery area, there are only a limited number of days in the year in which the height of the seas would allow even the best-designed ship to perform its task. The *Hughes Glomar Explorer* had to be on station in July and its task done by August. Later, water and weather conditions would deteriorate to a point from which further exploration would be impossible. This timetable could be used as a deadline to encourage workers as well as lend additional credence to the mining operations story.

Another major benefit from this mining cover from the government's point of view, was the very strong position being taken by the developing or third-world nations on control of all sea-floor prospecting.

It was clear the U.S. Government, unless it wanted to establish a policy which would find immediate and vehement disfavour among these countries, as well as provide the Soviets with fine propaganda materials, could in no way be associated with a commercial seabed undertaking. But what if a private concern were found to come forward and act as a blind?

Project Jennifer would then have the perfect cover-up, one which would fit every requirement. It would also gain the added advantage of putting even more space between the CIA and the vessel about to be constructed.

There was also an additional benefit. The State Department, by inaction, could have a test case on sea-floor development and law. A commercial concern, albeit American, could hardly be attacked in the U.N. There would be an opportunity to see just who lined up where, and how fast, as well as to establish a very good precedent which would have a powerful effect when used in future negotiations. The American form of government is supportive of private enterprise.

To raise no suspicions, the private company needed to be one which, logically, might go exploring for minerals on the ocean floor.

The Summa Corporation (then called Hughes Tool Company), headquartered in Las Vegas, Nevada, was the perfect choice. The company already had an established undersea minerals division, it had a certain closeness to the CIA and its sole stockholder was a man named Howard R. Hughes.

7

Howard Hughes is a name with which to conjure. Pilot, golfer, industrialist, motion picture producer and director, builder of empires and the world's most famous recluse. Not to mention one of its very richest men.

Hughes played a very direct role in the Jennifer Project. Without him and his companies, it would never, in all likelihood, have happened. Intricacies of his involvement with many high government officials are still, at the time of this writing, being uncovered. But it is necessary to try to deal with some of these relationships to present the Jennifer story in full.

Since it's almost impossible to follow the Hughes saga without some base of understanding of his far-flung empire, an outline of the Summa Corporation and its holdings is needed. The Summa Corporation was formed in December 1972, when Hughes sold, to his key men and then to the public, the total assets of the Hughes Tool Company. This corporate entity retained the name Hughes Tool and brought a reported $150 million into Howard Hughes' empire. All other companies which he owned and controlled were merged into a single entity, called Summa – the highest.

Howard Hughes held no corporate office in this company, nor was he a director of the firm. He was, simply enough, the sole stockholder. Many of his managers, who never saw him in person, referred to him as 'the Shareholder.'

Summa was one of two entities which Hughes held. He was also sole trustee of the Howard Hughes Medical Institute. The importance the Medical Institute has to the Jennifer Project is its relationship to Hughes Aircraft.

The Howard Hughes Medical Institute has two major holdings: The Hughes Aircraft Company, which manufactures missiles, space and electronic equipment, and through Hughes Aircraft the institute controls 50% of the stock of Theta Cable Television.

Summa is more diverse and complex. First, the company has an estimated $2,000,000 in cash. But this asset is dwarfed by the amounts of money in the Hughes Nevada Operations, which include the Sands, Frontier, Desert Inn, Landmark and Castaways hotels, as well as the Paradise Valley Country Club, Harold's Club and the Silver Slipper Casino. All these establishments have legal gambling, and the daily cash flow is astronomical.

Then, in no particular order, Summa also owns Hughes Helicopters, a major manufacturer of military airlift equipment; Hughes Television Network, which ties together local stations to provide special network programming for spectacular events; TV station KLAS in Las Vegas; Hughes Air West, a small airline serving the western U.S. and Mexico with regularly scheduled flights; several gold and silver mining interests; Hughes Aviation Services, a company specializing in aircraft maintenance and special terminal facilities for charter flights; Archisystems, a firm to provide architectural expertise; and, finally, many square miles of real estate in Nevada, Arizona and Southern California.

Operating through four divisions, one for each of its major areas of interest, Summa exerts a great deal of influence and control throughout the world. And it has a long record of doing business with the Federal Government.

Howard Hughes started with a company worth about

65

$750,000 in 1924 and built it into the empire just described. The Howard Hughes Medical Institute is run like no other non-profit, private foundation. It gives no grants, employing instead 'medical investigators' in various locations. The government has been engaged in a long-term running battle with the institute over its status as a tax-free trust, the main points of contention being Hughes' tight control and the institute's close ties with Hughes Aircraft Company. Thus far, all challenges by the government to the tax-free status have failed.

With the empire in mind, let's look at some little-known facts about the man who built it, and at some of the individuals he appointed to serve as his executives.

Howard R. (for Robard, a name he never used) Hughes was born on Christmas Eve 1905 in Houston, Texas, at 1402 Crawford, a rented house on a dirt street.

His father, Howard, Sr., was an inventive man of great mechanical curiosity. Experienced in mining engineering, he had devised the rotary bit and several other advances and innovations in the equipment used to drill for oil. (It is no more than a coincidence, but it is interesting that Hughes grew up surrounded by the industrial technology which was to play a major part in the Jennifer Project.) The elder Hughes' inventions had led him to the formation of Hughes Tool Company, a firm which exists today as a major supplier of oil field technology, and by the time of his son's birth he was well established financially.

Hughes Senior and Junior were fast friends. Young Howard was encouraged to exercise his inherited mechanical ability and sense of scientific curiosity. Before he was 15, he had made a radio transmitter, a motor for his bicycle, was a member of the then popular Radio Relay League and had taken his first airplane flight.

When he was 16, his mother, Alene, died. About two years later, just after he entered the freshman class at Rice Institute in Houston, Texas, his father passed away.

Hughes immediately left college and assumed control of his father's sizable business. He soon exhibited his desire for total control by buying out his relatives' shares. Hughes Tool prospered along with the rest of the petroleum industry in the area, and just before his 21st birthday, he turned down an offer of $7.5 million for the company.

Restless, he began seeking new fields to conquer.

By 1925, the impact of the motion picture was being felt throughout America, and the most glamorous place in the country was Hollywood.

Howard Hughes took the town by storm, and in six years produced a great many films. 'Hell's Angels' shocked the movie industry with its production budget, which went to $4 million when it was almost totally redone to add sound. The same picture introduced his protege Jean Harlow to a waiting public. Later 'Scarface,' starring Paul Muni in his first major role, set the tone for a rash of gangster pictures. Others of Hughes' films, including his first, 'Swell Hogan,' said to be so poor it was never released, were less attractive at the box office. Hughes seemed to specialize in taking unknown performers and, through publicity coupled with daring or good roles, making them into celebrities.

Hughes lived simply during this period, residing mostly in rented houses and apartments. Although he took no real part in movie world society, he was linked romantically with several women. Hughes, by this time, had been married to and divorced (after four and a half years) from the former Ella Rice of Houston, who was a daughter of the founding family of Rice Institute.

After a few years, the attraction of the movies began to pale on this by now extremely wealthy young man, and he began to look for new skies. His friend, adviser and employee, Noah Dietrich, said, 'Howard wanted to achieve three things. He wanted to be the world's greatest golfer, the world's best aviator and the world's richest man. We've got a start on the third one.'

Hughes' interest in golf, while brief, was, as might be expected, intense. But his real avocation was aviation.

Hughes learned to fly during the filming of his first success, 'Hell's Angels' (he later made several other pictures with airplanes). He also had the first of his many aircraft accidents; the World War I fighter plane in which he was training went out of control and crashed. But he persevered and went on to become a highly skilled, somewhat daring pilot.

Aviation was in a low period between the two wars, not yet a proven commercial industry but obviously more than a novelty circus act.

Hughes established an aviation company devoted to experimental and high performance concepts, and from 1935 to 1939, he gained great notice and fame as a master pilot. Among his achievements are the land flying speed record of 352 miles per hour set in 1935, and the 1936 flight which won him the Harmon Trophy for setting a cross-country speed record (which he broke by a wide margin the following year). In 1938, in a Lockheed monoplane (it's interesting to see how far back Hughes' relationship with Lockheed goes) he flew 14,716 miles around the earth in a record time of under 3 days, 19 hours, making only 6 stops. In the period 1935-1938 he set three major speed records and won the coveted Harmon Trophy two times.

A daring man, Hughes was also a careful and exact planner. To his mind, his flights were not done as stunts but as scientific endeavours, and he planned and checked every facet personally. One of the stories indicative of his concern for detail was the series of experiments he ran to determine which bread would stay fresh longest, so his sandwiches would have more taste on the long hops.

Among his many real aviation contributions was the testing of the Sperry Gyro-Pilot and a line-of-position computer. Both were successfully demonstrated to be effective, worthwhile aids to aviation.

After receiving the Harmon Trophy and the Collier Trophy for his around-the-world performance, he drifted away from flying and returned to Houston, where he devoted his attention to Hughes Tool.

Hollywood again, however, exerted a strong pull on him, and he returned to produce one of the most controversial pictures of its time, 'The Outlaw.' For the film, Hughes is said to have designed a special uplift brassiere, intended to improve Jane Russell's already ample cleavage.

The Second World War brought new opportunities for Hughes, now a major U.S. industrialist, to advance flying and at the same time develop Hughes Aircraft into one of the nation's biggest Defense Department suppliers. He was stopped for a brief time due to another crash, in May 1943, but was soon back to his almost ceaseless work schedule.

In addition to developing several unique reconnaissance aircraft, it was about this point in time when serious design work started on the HK-1, popularly called the 'Spruce Goose.'

Hughes, concerned with the horrifying loss of U.S. and other allied troop and supply ships to torpedoes from the dreaded German U-boats, conceived the idea of a massive transport aircraft capable of carrying large numbers of men and literally tons of equipment. His plan was to at least partially replace surface shipping by an airlift.

The result of his speculation was the largest amphibian aircraft ever constructed. Built entirely of wood, because of the wartime shortage of metal, and powered by eight engines, the finished plane was larger than a modern Boeing 747. It could take off and land from the water, so as to allow it to operate from facilities anywhere in the world and give access to the already developed seaport materials-handling systems for rapid loading and unloading. Work on the project continued long after the *Enola Gay* had spelled an end to the war in a devastating atomic bomb attack on Hiroshima. In fact, the 'Spruce Goose' was not ready to fly until 1947, when Hughes was involved in a life-altering event.

From his earlier flamboyant behaviour, it was apparent Howard Hughes realized the value of publicity. At times he seemed to crave it for its own sake, and certainly seemed to enjoy even staged events such as the receiving of his 1937 flying award from Franklin Delano Roosevelt, then President of the United States, and the ticker-tape parade down Broadway on his return from his globe-spanning 1938 flight. But the war years, for the most part, put an end to press coverage of his feats of aviation and of speculation on his relationships with the world's most beautiful women.

Eyewitness accounts, however, of all his personal appearances agree on one point. Even while in the limelight, he exhibited a shy, withdrawn manner.

The publicity he received in 1947 was of a very different nature. A Congressional subcommittee including Senator Owen Brewster of Maine began an investigation of his wartime contracts, and finally charged Hughes Aircraft with profiteering from the manufacture of planes and other materials. Hughes was said to have won a special $70 million contract for his unique reconnaissance airplane by lavishly entertaining high-ranking military officers. Included in the allegations was the specific charge of procuring women for sexual purposes for a number of key people.

Hughes was both surprised and shocked at the quick pick-up of the seamier sides of the story by the press and by the media's adverse attitude towards him. Still in a less than perfect physical state due to his long recovery from the most serious crash of his career, he mustered all his considerable personal forces and, backed by an effective team of advisers and attorneys, successfully defended himself in the round of hearings. He emerged vindicated, if not exonerated.

His performance before the committee was dramatic and powerful. Showing a side rarely seen in public, he was dynamically brilliant in his handling of Brewster and the other members critical of his actions, and revealed to even a casual observer the keenness of his mind and his great capability to attend to details. And though he emerged the victor, his pride was hurt on two counts. The first he resolved immediately.

Allegations had been made in the press during the hearings, based on information made public by the Congressional committee, that the 'Spruce Goose' was a total and complete boondoggle. It was called 'the most expensive pile of scrap lumber in history' and serious questions were asked about its ability to even get off the ground. In an act much in keeping with the Hughes personality of this era, he publicly vowed to fly the HK-1 or leave the country.

After several months of intensive preparation, and observed by newsreel cameras as well as representatives from the worldwide press, Hughes, on November 2, 1947, fired up the eight powerful engines. Taxiing out into the waters off Long Beach, with spray flying, he pulled the giant seaplane up to an altitude of 70 feet and held her there for a mile. After a less than cushiony landing, in another cloud of spray, he shut her down and walked away, never to publicly return.

The second hurt to Hughes' pride was not so easily or publicly rectified. He felt, according to his close associates, he had been singled out unfairly and made a fool of in the popular press. His honour and his sense of justice were injured.

After contemplating the matter, he came up with a solution which would provide him with both additional profits, as well as protection against future occurrences of the same type of embarrassment. He launched a programme to entangle the affairs of Hughes Aircraft and himself with the most clandestine elements of the government.

In addition to taking his first real look at the mechanisms of American politics and the effects of money on the system, he used his wartime contacts to begin the development of an alliance with the top-secret side of the U.S. Defense Department.

During World War II, Hughes Aircraft had begun an enduring interest in the design and manufacture of exotic weapons systems and would become, in time, one of the Pentagon's primary contractors for experimental and secret equipment. Under Hughes' guidance, the aircraft company became the centre of advanced concept and design of electronics weaponry and other military electronic applications. One example of a Hughes success was the development of the first laser-beam generating equipment.

Hughes, while lacking in technical education, was an inveterate experimenter, and often proceeded in a direction selected because of a hunch or inspiration. On more than one occasion he caused major trouble among the staff scientists, who disliked his sometimes uninformed second-guessing of their research. Things at one point got so bad the Pentagon had to step in as referee, and Hughes was eventually forced to remove himself from the scene by creating the nonprofit Hughes Medical Institute as a buffer between himself and the Hughes Aircraft staff.

Obviously, the real reason for this move was to save taxes, but it came at a time of peak pressure from the Air Force, and Hughes showed his creative ability by turning its threats to withdraw research contracts into an excuse to save himself millions of dollars annually.

The list of Hughes Aircraft successes is impressive. Scientists there designed the signal-amplifying microwave tubes, first used in the U.S. surveillance satellites and now found in commercially available equipment. And the company's work with synchronous orbit satellites and the moon landing surveyor spacecraft are foundation stones of the U.S. space effort. Hughes Aircraft also excels in electronic weaponry design. In addition to fire control systems and missiles, three-dimensional radar,

now also used commercially, came from this
company.

As the years passed, Hughes became more wit,
and reclusive, and more secretive towards the publi
his business dealings and personal affairs. But his c
for doing business improved, apparently, along w
driving desire for control of all he touched, which led
him to perfect the use of political contributions. Hughes
is reported to have contributed up to $400,000 a year to
politicians running for everything from county com-
missioner to President, but like most of his dealings, his
political activities were held in strict secrecy.

It is apparent these donations required huge amoun
of money, preferably in small denominations. And the
was no better place to generate this kind of cash than
gambling casino. Hughes had his choice of several,
could, if he'd wished, have taken a little from each
make the loss more difficult to trace.

Howard Hughes had started on a path which w
eventually make him the world's most famous re
The only time he ever spoke publicly about his
drawal was in a meeting with the U.S. Ambassa
Nicaragua, Shelton Turner. He is quoted as say
was working on inventions and making plans, h
and visitors kept interrupting me. So I instru
aides to cut down on appointments and calls
gradual, but I finally realized I wasn't seeing
probably carried things too far.' He was
laughing as he finished the statement.

Three airplane smashups had left him wit
deafness and marred the strong features
Worse, on one of his high-altitude globe-cir
he'd been forced to breathe oxygen through
for a long period of time. Above Siberia, th
tube conducted the cold and froze his ja
bone disease. Over a period of time, this b
his jaw line.

How large a part vanity played in his

to assess. But another, much clearer factor was his ∎ire to dominate the people around him and his fear of being dominated or having others gain power over him in any way. He demanded a total obedience to his orders, including his whims and fancies. Few could tolerate the totality of his attitude.

Actress Jean Peters, who married Hughes in 1957, lived for fourteen years in partial isolation, surrounded 24 hours a day by maids and servants whom she knew were reporting back to her husband. Finally, she had enough and divorced him. The settlement was reported to have included $50,000 a year for life. Hughes was now 66 years old and set in his ways. The divorce seems to have cut his final ties with the conventions of the real world, and he became even more of a recluse.

He'd already managed to set some records in this area. His last published photo, taken in 1952, was nineteen years old, and no one had seen him in public since 1958. The only halfway factual report on his life style came from an eyewitness who was forced to testify in 1971 in a legal suit in Nevada.

The man, Howard Eckersley, said Hughes had locked himself into total isolation. According to Eckersley, Hughes had moved into one room of the Desert Inn penthouse, and was completely sheltered from outsiders by a team of five nurse-aides. Four of the team were members of the Church of the Latter Day Saints and the fifth was married to a Mormon. Hughes seems to have had a real sense of trust in members of this church. Several high-ranking members of his staff are also of the same persuasion. His propensity for the followers of the Mormon faith seems to have been based on the belief that these people would be less susceptible to bribes and other inducements to discuss his actions with outsiders. Equally important, he appears to have felt the members of this church would be less inclined to attempt to influence him.

Hughes' one-room existence was as close to solitary

confinement as a man could possibly get. All windows were shuttered by black drapes, taped down so as to admit no light. For years, a glass wall separated the room from the rest of the apartment, to fend off external germs.

All his communication was by telephone or hand-written memos, which he would pass out to the waiting nurse-aides or hold up to the glass partition for them to read. Most of the time, he sat in a straightbacked chair, usually clad in pyjamas, and gave weird written commands, such as, 'Please watch me carefully, and do not let me go to sleep at all.'

The CIA, in contacting Hughes, was treading a familiar route. He and his staff, which was rife with ex-members of the CIA and FBI, worked hand in glove with the members of the cloak-and-dagger gang. Hughes had been an active favourite to call upon for special projects since the Office of Strategic Services (OSS) days of World War II. And this relationship had grown until, in places, it was hard to tell where the Hughes organization ended and the CIA began.

His involvement in the Bay of Pigs fiasco is well documented. He provided a small island off Florida as a training area to carry out invasion exercises. One of the cadre of instructors on Cay Sal, Gary Hemming, an ex-Marine, recalled to the press he'd helped unload boxes of supplies which had 'Toolco' markings on the outside. 'Toolco' is the trade name for Hughes Tool.

Hughes Aircraft, during the period 1965-1975, had a reported $6 billion in defence contracts and an estimated additional $6 billion in secret CIA-based business.

There was no doubt to whom the CIA would turn in an effort to find the right firm to help cover the hardware for Project Jennifer. But a slip did occur, when it was decided to go to the top and deal only with the man himself, due to the sensitive nature of the project.

The direct contact to Hughes was attempted and soundly rebuffed. Which was not surprising, considering President Nixon himself considered Hughes as independent as a foreign government. After due deliberation, the agency redirected its efforts, and in 1969, going through channels, approached Raymond Holliday, then the chief executive director of Hughes Tool. When he heard the details of the CIA proposal, he agreed to approach Hughes.

In a short time, Holliday notified the CIA of Hughes' permission to use his name and company as cover, on 'the collection effort for the submarine.' Several memos to this effect seem to have been written by Hughes and his staff.

Even the most cursory review of the records indicates a close and long-standing relationship between Howard Hughes and the CIA. And, based upon Hughes' quoted statement to his then trusted aide Robert Maheu, a major motive for his friendly involvement, aside from the millions of dollars in special contracts, was his feeling he would never again be confronted with a serious government-backed investigation.

He knew too much to be questioned about anything. From the fact he never again made a court appearance, it appears he may have been right.

According to informed sources in Houston, Texas, where his body was taken and finally buried, Howard Hughes died of kidney misfunction while in his ultra-private penthouse on the 20th floor of the pyramid-shaped Princess Hotel in Acapulco, Mexico. Because of possible problems with the notoriously corrupt Acapulco police and probable red tape of the Mexican government, a tourist card was forged with his signature and his remains were spirited out of the country aboard a Lear Jet chartered from Florida. The cover story of his death en route was formed to smooth over future difficulties with Mexican authorities.

His death ended the involved, unusual career of a strong, determined man. Hughes considered himself first and foremost a patriot. Seen from his viewpoint, while remembering he was a man certain of his power and wisdom, many of his less understandable acts become rational. He was an individual with a rare mental make-up. The same brilliance which made him, trapped him.

He isolated himself for considering a single problem and making an effective decision. But before he could recover, because of his depth of involvement in all phases of his business, another crucial deciding point had been reached. So he remained isolated, as one challenge with a dire need of immediate decision came hot on the heels of another.

The isolation became routine; from routine, came habit. And habit, in a person of iron will, becomes inflexible rule.

Howard Robard Hughes left gigantic footprints across the fabric of the social order in which he lived.

Even in death, he is consistent. The world's most famous millionaire is buried in a plot in an old cemetery in Houston, Texas, alongside his father and mother. For a long while, the grave remained unmarked. As in his life, there was no testimony to his presence. His obsession for privacy had finally been fulfilled to the maximum.

8

Hughes' permission to use his corporation as cover for Jennifer resulted in immediate action. By January 1970, the CIA, using the Hughes name, was deep into its work with many contractors, including Global Marine and Lockheed.

Lockheed's relationship with the Hughes organization goes back many years, and its reputation for discretion in carrying out defence contracts was tried and proven.

Global Marine was another matter. It has been mistakenly reported Hughes controlled the company. This is not true. The company was formed in 1958, when a group of employees bought their organization from Union Oil. Through a combination of good business management and really innovative technological advances in what was then a relatively unsophisticated industry, the company prospered and has been listed on the New York Stock Exchange since 1967. The company reported revenues of $89.1 million in 1974, and as of March 1975, operated 20 drilling vessels worldwide. Generally, inside the oil industry, Global Marine is noted for its excellent technology and staff, and its sometimes lower than average profits.

The growth of the company was based on two areas of endeavour. First, it was active in deep-water drilling for oil and gas. And secondly, it held, as a subsidiary, a long-range weather forecasting service. In 1976, it owned 15 drilling vessels, and its list of clients included the U.S. Navy as well as most of the major oil companies. Global Marine is also known to have worked under contract with the Soviets.

While it had not had the same long-time relationship with the Hughes interests as did Lockheed, it was not unknown to the Hughes people, having been a customer of Hughes Tool for drilling bits and other equipment. D. W. Williams, an ex-Rice football great and a one-time vice president of Global Marine, based in Houston, was a personal friend of Raymond Holliday. Informed sources indicate Williams played a major role in inducing Hughes Tool to assign the development of the *Hughes Glomar Explorer* to GMI.

As things turned out, Global Marine was an excellent choice. They could provide both the expertise and technology required to design and oversee the construction of the special ship and, because of their experience in oil exploration, could offer sound guidance for the operation of the vessel.

But the ship was only one of many major construction projects to be undertaken. Final plans called for several components. In addition to the work vessel, there was the pipe for the string. And some kind of a claw or grapple, along with its controls, to lock onto the pieces of the sub. Finally, the project would require a special drydock type of barge, which could be submerged, to aid in fitting the claw.

Global Marine was named prime contractor, and it turned to Lockheed and Hughes Tool for manufacturing and technical assistance. Lockheed's Ocean Systems Division, using aerospace technology, took on the job of laying out the barge and, more importantly, the claw. Several other firms were also involved, due to the complexity of the electronic gear and the sophistication of the equipment to be installed on the main vessel.

The actual construction of the *Hughes Glomar Explorer*

was by the Sun Shipbuilding & Dry Dock Company in their Chester, Pennsylvania, shipyards, under an April 1971 contract. The ship was launched in November 1972.

The 41 months required for its concept, design, working plans and construction is considered to be a very short time for such a project. It was possible only because of the careful planning by the Global Marine task force.

The launching of the ship, in Chester, was heralded by a special 'Family Day' party for the workers at the yards. A handbill was printed advertising 'Refreshments and Balloons,' and on November 4, 1972, a great many people saw the top-secret vessel up close.

The barge and claw were built in the same time frame. Actual construction of the *HMB-1* (Hughes Marine Barge), as the barge was officially called, was by the National Steel & Shipbuilding Corporation, in their San Diego, California, yards. The immense size of the barge, and the need to coordinate its completion with the much more difficult task of constructing the claw, strongback and controls, made the project a difficult one. The claw system fabrication work took place on the barge at Lockheed's Redwood City facility, and involved more than 300 men who knew it was to be used on a secret government mission.

The special lift pipe required a great amount of time to produce. Each 30-foot piece was individually forged from the type of steel used in cannon barrels, and then stress-tested to loads exceeding 24 million pounds. The expertise of Hughes Tool Company was called upon to its fullest, and it met every aspect of its contract with Global Marine on time and on spec.

The coordination was beautiful, and the completed pipe string was ready to be installed below decks on the main vessel shortly after its arrival in California.

The security problem involved in the project was, by now, reaching record proportions. A study of the cover story, along with the precautions taken to avoid leaks, will set the stage for the actual recovery effort, as well as explain several things which occurred after the real story was leaked in the press.

Once the initial equipment requests were made to the suppliers of the hundreds of components the mission would require, the need for a public announcement of the cover story was urgent. Like most of Howard Hughes' publicity efforts, it was a bang-up job. The undersea mining venture became common knowledge overnight.

The initial story, as released, was simple and characteristically direct. Summa Corporation, and therefore Howard Hughes, on a private venture basis, was going to attempt to harvest nodules of solid metal from the sea floor. To do so, they would need a special ship, the construction of which was under way. A barge, to be used as a service vehicle, would also be required.

Two steps were taken to be certain the story gained maximum exposure. First, Summa Corporation, through its regular publicity release channels, started a major campaign complete with articles in technical and business publications. Its position was strictly one of a profit-making organization attempting a new and daring challenge. Subcontractors were given separate stories about their contributions, and the sea floor was widely claimed to be the new mining frontier.

Then, to give additional credence to the plan, actual agreements, such as the one with American Smelting & Refining to process recovered ore, were negotiated with several companies.

Business competition being what it is, it didn't take long for the major mineral producers, who felt themselves on a par with Summa in mining operations, to come forward with stories about plans of their own. Some were positive, and outlined slightly vague programmes supposedly under way for 'some time'; others were hostile and generally debated the entire commercial value of seabed prospecting. New departments called

81

'Oceanographic' or 'Ocean Resources' were created overnight to be competitive.

Regardless of the position taken, the stories from the other companies provided an air of legitimacy, and the more the idea was debated the more publicity was generated. *Business Week*, among other national magazines, carried a lengthy article on what effect the availability of pure nonferrous metal, picked up at very low cost, would have on prices. The editors, like many others, appeared to be taken in by the Summa Corporation-generated, CIA-backed campaign.

Once the main story had been printed in a number of U.S. publications, the CIA began its own international publicity effort. The goal, however, was not so much cover as it was to establish a *fait accompli* in the matter of third-world resistance to seabed exploration. The CIA's campaign centred on the entrepreneurial activities of Hughes and Summa.

The State Department, going along with the CIA effort (possibly originally requested by it as a side activity to the real Jennifer Project), took a position of noninvolvement. When questioned on official American policy, its response was 'our position is still under consideration.' As far as Summa and its announced plans were concerned, the executives in State merely shrugged. After all, America is a free country; the company is a private business and is free to conduct its affairs as it deems proper.

The publicity caused heavy international interest in the project and drew a surprising amount of comment. The alignment of many influential people and nations became clear and, for the first time, the U.S. could see where a great many friends positioned themselves on the issue of seabed regulation. This information proved valuable in future discussions.

Little of the international response reached the domestic press. A few news stories appeared, but they were a part of the total new-frontier theme which the CIA and

Summa moved into as soon as interest in the straight business theme of the first effort was exhausted. The technique of hiding something by placing it in full view was perfected during this phase of the operation, and the publicity even went so far as to create a mood of excitement about the actual vessel, calling it 'Howard Hughes' mystery ship.'

At every turn, the people who were working on the project, from those making the drawings all the way to the welders and fitters in the yard, were confronted with a public explanation for their activity. Since everyone knew Hughes was strange, the inordinate number of obvious G-man and intelligence types who came and went could easily be written off to the recluse's well-known love of secrecy.

An example of how effective the publicity effort was can be seen from the almost 4,000 people who were given a security oath or were checked for a clearance.

Four thousand is a lot of people. But by estimates from a reliable source, there were probably over 7,000 individuals who had some contact with the project during the construction phase. No one guessed, at the time, the nature of the mission. The cover was excellent.

It also provided another vital ingredient for the mission's success.

Since the vessel was going out to search for wealth on the sea floor, it would, of course, sail in secrecy. Understandably, since Summa would not wish the site of its exploration to become a matter of common knowledge, attempts to follow the *Hughes Glomar Explorer* could be discouraged.

Construction on *Explorer* continued at a hectic pace. The ship was launched in November in a semicompleted state, with only the hull, hull structure, inner bottom, wing wall, tunnel thrusters, shafts, motors, bilge and ballast in place. More than half the work was still to be done on the wire ways and hangers, the fireman or firefighting system and other crucial components.

Built without a keel because of the large opening in the bottom, the vessel required twelve months of work just to be made floatable. An additional eight months would be needed before Sun Shipbuilding would be finished with its job and transfer the ship to Global Marine's control.

Her first sea trials, in February and March 1973, found the vessel in excellent operating condition, needing only minor adjustments and modifications.

Finally, on July 23, Capt. James M. Miles, an experienced master mariner, took command and moved the vessel out into the Delaware River. In the bright, hot sunlight, the ship motored about a mile upstream, then turned and waited. Finally, at his order, they moved back downstream, under the high span of the steel bridge at Wilmington, to a selected anchorage, still in the protected waterway.

There the ship laid by for a number of days while the top of the derrick, too tall to clear the bridge, was installed and other finishing touches were completed. Then they turned east into the grey, rolling Atlantic for a month of sea trials.

During this period, the very unusual design of the ship and all the working components were exhaustively tested. One of the most novel features of the vessel was the 199-foot-long opening in the centre of the vessel. Called the 'Moon Pool,' this more than 12,000-square-foot tank was to be the heart of the recovery operation. In normal configuration, it was closed to the water by two steel doors or gates which retracted fore and aft into the hull. The claw, strongback and all ancillary equipment and attachments to the pipe string were to be carried in this area. During the actual recovery letdown of the lift pipe string, the pool would be flooded, the gates would slide back open to the water and the grapple would be lowered into the depths.

This same testing period was used to try the dynamic station-keeping capabilities of the vessel, as well as components of the heavy lift system.

A complete machine shop had been set up on board for on-the-spot fabrication to correct flaws found during the initial cruise, and the area towards the bow was equipped with a heavy-duty gantry crane. During the retrieval, this capability would be used to cut open the sub.

One point must be clearly established. The ship had been constructed for only one purpose. Each and every dimension, from the size of the Moon Pool to the number of men accommodated on board, had been calculated with a single job in mind. This is important, because later, when eyewitness information is provided on what was found, the very uniqueness of the ship's design and the clearness of intent are important to the substantiation of the reports.

Only a limited amount of information as to precisely where the vessel went during its maiden voyage is available. The sea trials had to include the operation of the entire ship as a system. One report indicates the vessel stationed itself near or over the site of the *Scorpion* disaster. This has never been verified. But such a positioning would have been of little practical use, as the lift string was still in the final stages of fabrication and was not aboard.

Regardless of where the ship sailed, she arrived in Bermuda about August 10 and there, after a brief layover to change crews, Capt. Elmer Thompson came aboard to assume command for the long journey to California. Most of the research and development staff disembarked at this time, and aside from the maritime crew, only a minimal number of people remained on board.

Further testing, rebuilding and construction were stopped during this transit run, and were not started again until the vessel reached its home port in Long Beach, California.

All published reports to the contrary, at no time during its sojourn in the Atlantic Ocean was the *Hughes Glomar Explorer* able to achieve its primary function. It was, at best, only partially finished. Both the lift pipe and the huge underwater machine the lift pipe was designed to carry were just nearing completion. Final drawings for several details of the ship itself were still in process. And the barge, launched some months prior to the ship and field-tested in Isthmus Cove, off Santa Catalina Island, in February 1972 was snug in its berth in Redwood City, California. Since the barge and the claw were vital parts of the total operations package, there was no way the ship could have undertaken recovery work before its arrival in California on October 3, 1973.

By July 1974 the hardware was ready. It had taken years and millions of dollars to be developed and produced. It had involved thousands of people and massive construction on a scale uncommon in even a shipyard, and had stretched available technology to the very limits.

The justification for this time, money and effort was to be a single, winner-take-all dice roll, three miles down in the black depths of the blue Pacific, exploring where no man had explored before.

9

The *Hughes Glomar Explorer* was a special ship, on a special kind of mission. To be successful, several groups with different skills were needed to make up the complement of her crew.

First, there were the traditional seamen, in charge of sailing the ship, all operations at sea and maintenance of the vessel itself. This group consisted of the ship's master, his mates, electricians, the engine room crew, the deck hands and the stewards. Their number was more heavily composed of individuals with training in stationary power generators and refrigeration than would be found in a normal crew. These men lived somewhat apart from the rest and worked the bell-divided traditional seagoing shifts.

Then there were the scientists and technicians. This group was split between those responsible for some part of the actual recovery try, such as monitoring the claw or taking stress readings on the pipe string, and those assigned to assess the materials brought to the surface.

A smaller sub-group, attached to the scientific community by their backgrounds and to the nautical group because of their duties, was formed by the meteorologists, communications technicians and experts in sonar and other undersea surveillance methods as well as computer maintenance.

87

A contingent of the CIA was also included, as more or less supervisory personnel to maintain security and oversee the total operation. An extra-large housekeeping crew, part of the maritime group and consisting of cabin stewards, cooks, and bottle washers, provided a necessary backup for everyone on board.

All of the above number were male. Many were members of the United States Navy on assignment or leave of absence. The pipe handlers, welders and rig men were all civilians of diverse ages but similar backgrounds. They had been recruited with great care by the CIA, which used a special hiring office on the fifth floor of the Tishman Building at 5959 Century Boulevard in Los Angeles and branch offices in Houston, Texas, and other Gulf Coast cities.

On one wall of the California interview room was a picture of the *Hughes Glomar Explorer*. Sample manganese nodules, supposedly the target for the ship's mining gear, were placed strategically about. The nodules were authentic. *Seascope*, another Global Marine-designed vessel, had been leased in the fall of 1971, at Global Marine's suggestion, to gather a few thousand pounds of the black lumps to lend credence to the cover story. *Seascope* sailed from Santa Barbara and returned with less than twenty tons of nodules.

Each of the men was given a very tight security check, using the known eccentricities of Howard Hughes as an excuse. One example of the CIA's thoroughness was the payment of $25 a month to each candidate who was to be examined, so as to prevent invasion-of-privacy suits.

Recruited one at a time, both for their ability to be cleared and their expertise as crane operators, rig handlers, welders, cutting torch operators, etc., they were told they would serve for an indefinite length of time after an intensive period of special schooling.

These men brought aboard with them the basic rules of conduct they had learned the hard way while working on the huge offshore platforms in the Gulf of Mexico.

They knew arguments between individuals started in off-hours might carry over into their shift, and a minor disagreement could produce disaster through a single second's inattention.

Their code was simple: On shore, anything goes; on the rig or the boat, no drinking, no gambling and no petty annoyances. Every man conducted himself in such a fashion as not to bother anyone else on board. Even in their conversations over coffee they seemed guarded, careful not to say anything anyone might find offensive. The combination of long hours and heat, mixed with the ever-present dangers inherent in their routines, produced explosive tempers. No one wanted to be the fuse. The main subjects for conversation, considered safe by everyone, dealt with past jobs and future prospects.

This group lived in relative isolation, in a special area established for their use. Numerically, they were a minority. As few as 20, according to some reports, but surely no more than 40, counting the superintendents who oversaw both shifts. There were more than twice as many scientists and engineers on board, and the housekeeping crew, including food personnel, easily exceeded them in number.

The design of the vessel had included the need for crew segregation to provide some degree of secrecy during the examination and evaluation of the recovered materials. A quick tour through the ship and reference to the diagram will show how this was done.

Starting at the very rear of the vessel, the helicopter pad extends back, out over the edge of the bridge deck, and is large enough to accommodate landings and take-offs by even the biggest choppers operating today.

Forward of this are the bridge and wheelhouse, the radio room, the captain's office, his stateroom, two cabins with complete baths, the emergency generator room, the electric workshop and the chart room. The actual conning of the ship is performed in this area, and the cabins house ship's officers, including the navigator and first mate.

Down one level is the superstructure deck. The rear of this area contains a special office for the owner of the vessel and a well-appointed owner's stateroom. (When Howard Hughes owned TWA, a small group of seats was reported to be roped off on every flight, in case he might want to use them. There is a striking similarity between that usage, and the construction and naming of an area as 'The Owner's,' especially when the floor plan has no other quarters on this deck. The only other facilities are for two offices and a storage area. The owner would thus be assured of complete privacy.)

The next lower area, the boat deck, is given over to crew quarters. It is made up of 18 rooms for two men each, a superintendent's room, the chief engineer's quarters and storage lockers for dirty and clean linens. The need for clean linens and the necessity of supplying a storage area for them is but one example of the problems of supplying a large group of people confined to a limited space. The boat deck also is the location of 25-man inflatable life rafts for emergency use.

The poop deck is next. At the stern end, the anchor and the electric anchor windlass are attached to the superstructure. Forward, six rooms, designed to house four men each, are located next to a very large lounge area, a huge dining room, a scullery for dishwashing, a galley, a dry storage area, a six-man hospital, a doctor's office and a small but very complete surgery.

The lounge area has very complete recreational facilities. In addition to game tables and easy chairs, there are TV sets which play specially recorded video tapes of all top shows; a complete gymnasium with weights, punching bags and accessories; a movie screen and projector; Ping-Pong tables and other amenities to provide for the off-duty pastimes of a small army. According to some reports, the porno film *Deep Throat* was included in the viewing library.

90

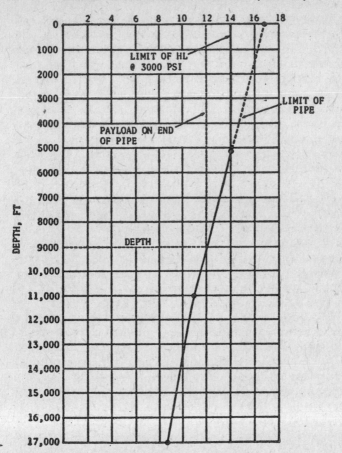

MAXIMUM PAYLOAD HANDLING CAPABILITY (LBS.X10⁶)

LIMIT OF HL @ 3000 PSI

PAYLOAD ON END OF PIPE

LIMIT OF PIPE

DEPTH

DEPTH, FT

PIPE STRING

MATL: 4330V MOD (GUN BARREL STL)
YLD: 150 - 165 KSI
ULT: 160 - 175 KSI

ALLOW TENSILE STR: 106 KSI
STOWED IN 60 FT DOUBLES

91

The twelve-hour work shifts placed a special demand on the cooks and their helpers. Meals were served four times a day, once every six hours and, since what was dinner to some was breakfast to others, three menus had to be offered at each service. In addition, on a twenty-four-hour basis, an assortment of snacks, coffee, juices and soft drinks was readily available

Because food is an area of possible discontentment among personnel on shipboard, the entire mess team was specially selected for the ability to provide not only gourmet dishes but also to cook regional gumbos, chilies and stews on request. A typical dinner offering consisted of roast beef, lobster tails, various vegetables, potatoes, salad and, to top it off, homemade breads and cakes. Rice, for the men from the Gulf Coast, was available for every meal, as was the Southern corn-based speciality, grits. Tabasco sauce was in constant demand.

The main deck of the vessel is made up of maintenance areas and shops for the carpenters, electricians and hydraulics engineers. Quarters are provided for 36 men, in 9 rooms.

The decks below this are laid out for storage, the ship's steering gear, a large generator room, the thruster room and the powerful thruster motors.

This deck arrangement runs from the stern of the ship forward about one-third of the way, where it is interrupted by the 199-foot-long opening of the Moon Pool. This provides a natural fore-and-aft barrier or division of the vessel. Filled with sea water, the Moon Pool looks like a huge swimming tank, except above decks a crane sits at each corner and the whole affair is topped by the huge A-frame supporting the stable platform and pipe-handling derrick.

Two other items of interest are in this area. The ship is equipped with a pair of decompression chambers, painted a bright, almost luminescent orange, for use by divers who have been down too deep or too long. These round, pressurized containers are used when there is a possibility of an oversaturation of nitrogen in a diver's blood, caused by pressure of the water. When the diver returns to normal surface pressure, the gas actually forms bubbles in his bloodstream, resulting in the dreaded 'bends.' Without treatment, the afflicted diver would die in agony in a matter of hours. The decompression chambers provide a pressurized environment which holds the gas in suspension in the blood. Then, as the nitrogen is gradually absorbed into the system over a period of hours, the pressure is slowly lowered until it is safe for the diver to return to a normal environment. The presence of two such devices indicates a considerable amount of deep diving was a planned portion of the exercise.

Forward of the Moon Pool, in the remaining third of the ship, is another multi-deck layer of shops and accommodations, contained in the forward housetop. The deck area in this section was used to hold 20 portable vans. Each contained a complete laboratory setup, and had its own hookup for air, power and water.

A huge gantry crane occupies the main deck between the edge of the pool and the superstructure. This crane, which has a 20-ton capacity, can be used for elaborate fabrications or to hold large items while they are being cut apart.

On the bridge deck of the forward housetop, there are a second captain's stateroom, the pilot house and three two-man staterooms. On the next level, the poop deck, are quarters for the maritime crew and their own galley, scullery, dining hall and lounge area. These facilities, although identical in equipment to those in the aft part of the ship, are somewhat smaller and designed to accommodate fewer people.

Below the poop deck are additional storage and the engines for the front thrusters.

The most surprising aspects of the ship are its size and variety of colour. From a distance, the vessel appears white. But on board, everything is a mixture of yellows and oranges, backed by marine blue and grey paint and augmented by the deep, almost purple, blue of the sky and the blue tone of the water. The ship is a maze of ladders, perforated steel walkways, pipe hand-holds, steep steps and narrow passages. Great yellow triangular spires shoot up a hundred feet overhead from the plates of the sun-heated deck and are topped by the peak of the derrick 50 feet higher.

The separation, vertically by deck, and fore and aft by the Moon Pool, of the various crew members who performed different functions was a deliberately thought-out security device. With the addition of the mobile laboratory trailers in the open space just forward of the pool, maintenance of the separation policy was possible even during working hours.

The group composed of the crane operators, welders, cutting torch handlers and other skilled tradesworkers kept pretty much to themselves, living by their code of careful conduct. On the trip out to the site, they ran a few trials to check modifications and determine the working condition of the gear, but by and large they were in an off-duty status, with time to do some wandering on the vessel and to ask questions. Job talk was considered to be a safe area of conversation, and comments about some of the more exotic personalities on board, as long as they were limited to the scientific group, the CIA and the maritime crew, was even better.

Before their arrival on the site, they had a pretty good idea of what to expect. Several weeks of classes had been held in special quarters near Redwood City, California. Among the subjects covered were the Geneva Convention and undersea treaties, the handling of radioactive materials, the Russian alphabet so during dismantling they could call out the letters on various controls and objects to nearby language specialists who would then translate for them, and instructions on what they should do if they were boarded. (By sticking to the cover story of being a civilian vessel engaged in civilian pursuits, the

CIA contemplated no resistance if the Soviets resorted to force.)

One story from this classroom period is of the huge party, paid for by the CIA, which the 'class' held one evening near graduation. When it comes to drinking and general hell-raising, these men are the equal of any in the world and far more proficient than most. Somehow, a few local girls became involved. ('There's no sense drinkin' unless there's women and fightin',' is one way to say it.) Before the evening was over, CIA staff members assigned to monitor the party were alarmed by the general level of boisterousness and feared the police might be called. The men's patriotism was appealed to and things were quieted down without too many outsiders being bothered.

By the end of their special training, the men were as ready for what might face them as they'd ever be.

The target submarine was in three pieces, and, if on-site down-deep surveillance agreed with the information from the *Mizar* survey of four years earlier, each of the three segments was available for recovery

What would be found within them, no one knew. Educated guesses ran from ghosts to guided missiles.

From the very start, the CIA recognized the difficulty of maintaining secrecy among the rig hands. Their style of life on shore, looser and more inclined toward booze and baby-dolls, made them bad risks. As it turned out, the design of the vessel, which segregated them from the other staff aboard and appeared to bolster security, actually caused an overabundance of curiosity. In their search for safe topics of conversation, they turned, naturally, once the recovery started, to speculation on what was actually found. And this speculation, augmented by unauthorized visits to the various work stations on board, has provided an excellent picture of what took place.

A great deal of work was still needed on the ship and several months were required to complete every detail.

During this time, from September 30, 1973, through January 1974, many people came and went. The government personnel aboard varied from a low of about 20 people to highs of just over 100. The nautical crews, under Captains Miles, Thompson and Gresham, rotated aboard for 30-day hitches, to provide what assistance they could

Finally, in the spring of 1974, everything was in readiness and the ship made at least two, probably three, because of an hydraulic problem in the heavy lift system, sea trials. Her performance was monitored by CIA representatives, and at the conclusion of the series, she was accepted by the U.S. Government from Global Marine.

The game was afoot.

SSB G-I Class

1.   Series I Golf Class Submarine with the short-range SS-N-4 missile hatches open. The photo dates back to 1970, before modifications were carried out to the 'sail' or conning tower of this particular vessel. (US Navy photo)

2.   The modified sail of the Soviet Golf Class Series II, fitted with the superior SS-N-5 missile system. Note the periscope and other crew-related paraphernalia (lookout ports, ventilating fans, etc.) have been moved forward to make room for the new missile installation. Judging from the graininess of this, it is a major enlargement, taken from a very high altitude. This is the type of submarine recovered by the *Hughes Glomar Explorer*. (US Navy photo)

3.   The *Hughes Glomar Explorer* at the rendezvous site off Santa Catalina Island in May 1975. The pool of turbulence to the right of the bow of the ship is apparently caused by the submerged HMB-1. (*Los Angeles Times* photo)

4.   This photo of the HMB was taken off the coast of Santa Catalina Island. The sailboat in the lower left gives some idea of the size of the giant vessel. (*Offshore Magazine* photo)

5. The *Hughes Glomar Explorer*. The docking legs are in their 'up' or raised position, so the ship is ready to sail. (*Los Angeles Times* photo)

6. A detailed cut-away drawing of the *Hughes Glomar Explorer*, showing the various features of the ship. (*Offshore Magazine* drawing)

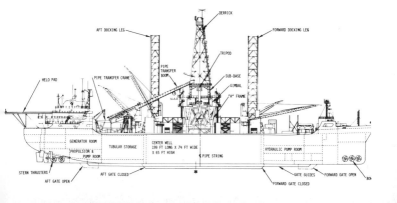

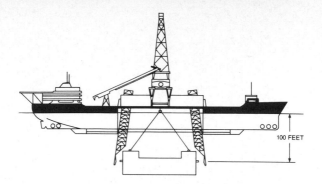

7.   This diagram shows how the docking legs lock onto a payload 100 feet below the surface, which allows transfer of major weights without disruption caused by ocean swells and shallow water effects. As the legs, patterned after the supports used on offshore drilling rigs, ascend, they carry the payload safely into the open Moon Pool. (*Offshore Magazine* drawing)

8.   The Long Base Line (LBL) Station Keeping System depends on an interrogation pulse that is sent from the *Hughes Glomar Explorer* to four transponders located on the floor of the ocean. These units send back a return pulse which is electronically interpreted to indicate how much the ship has moved from its original position.
The thrusters in the bow and stern allow the vessel to move sidways as well as to turn quickly, in response to position changes. (*Offshore Magazine* drawings)

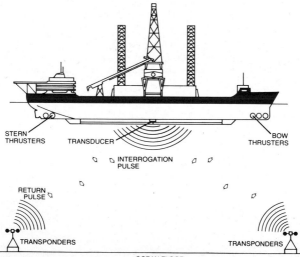

10

On July 4, 1974, the *Hughes Glomar Explorer*, with a crew of 172 carefully trained men and 80 days' lavish supplies, arrived at a point in the Pacific and began to take station. The selected site looked no different from any other square mile of the endless, rolling blue sea, but the instant satellite fixes supplied by the NAVSAT system said, 'This is the place,' and the ship hove to in almost 17,000 feet of water.

It had taken 20 months since the launching of the vessel to arrive at this particular spot in this vast ocean and, unlike the famous travel slogan, getting there had not been half the fun.

As a result of a series of events not directly concerned with the CIA, the Hughes organization, under investigation by the SEC, had suffered a break-in at one of their large record storage centres. Files pertaining to a pending SEC court hearing had been taken, along with a top secret memo to Hughes outlining Summa Corporation's involvement in the Jennifer Project.

The disappearance of this memo stating the true purpose of the *Hughes Glomar Explorer*'s mission sent the CIA officials into a state of shock. The ship had sailed by the time the loss of the memo was realized, and the top management of the CIA could only assume the worst. There was every possibility the Soviets knew of the voyage and were only waiting for the actual recovery to blow the whistle on the whole affair.

Finally, after days of agonizing discussion, the decision was made to continue the operation. The reasons behind this course, as well as a closer look at this aspect of the story, will be examined in a later chapter.

Suffice it to say, the men on board were working under an additional strain, compounded by the almost constant Soviet surveillance.

But strain was nothing new to the crew of the *Hughes Glomar Explorer*.

The ship had been through some of the roughest seas in the world. The Magellan Straits, north of the South Shetland Islands and south of Tierra Del Fuego is unlike any other place on our earth. At a latitude of 60 degrees, the sea and the air above it is dominated by the huge ice mass of the South Pole, just miles away. Strange winds arise, then die, only to arrive again from a totally different direction. Mists form in a matter of seconds and in minutes turn into dense fog, impenetrable by the human eye.

In the time of the sailing ships, this passage was feared by the seamen and officers alike. *HMS Bounty* tried for days to make it through, but the combination of errant and changing winds, along with the high seas, made turning back the only reasonable course.

The *Hughes Glomar Explorer* had a comparatively simple passage. The massive blades of her electrically powered propellers freed her from dependence on the winds and thus made the torturous channel less of a hazard. The crew, safe inside their steel cabins, surveyed the world through the electronic eyes of their radar. The rolling, pitching movement of the vessel was their worst hardship.

The project had also weathered a bizarre labour problem caused, at least partially, by the need for secrecy, and the continuation of work on major components of the ship.

The accommodations on board were unusual for an American merchant vessel. Engineers, who are allotted their own staterooms on most U.S. ships, were assigned two to a cabin because of the complex space requirements caused by the special components and the need to berth an unusually large number of people. This, coupled with wage disagreements and a lack of staffing of all recreational facilities, caused 10 members of the engineering crew to want to unionize the vessel and to have representation by the AFL/CIO Marine Beneficial Engineers Society.

The men in the engine room were a varied group, even for a private vessel. One was Australian born, three or four were recent graduates of the California State Maritime Academy and another was an ex-Coast Guardsman. Only one or two had any union experience at all, and the group was enthusiastic about their posts aboard the strange ship.

By the time they reached Long Beach, almost every member of the engineering crew, with the exception of the electricians, was ready to sign with the union.

It's not hard to imagine the CIA staff officers' reaction to this otherwise normal request, and the surprise of everyone at Global Marine's prompt dismissal of the ten activists.

The attorney for the union naturally took the matter through the regular legal channels, to be met with resistance on every hand. Global Marine was actually charged by the National Labour Relations Board (NLRB) for violations of the labour laws, but reported quick CIA action behind the scenes prevented the matter from being pursued as it could have been.

The vessel was picketed when it returned to port in 1974, and it's easy to imagine how funny the CIA thought that was. Here they were back from a secret mission, and there were men on the docks with placards and signs calling the attention of the press to their arrival.

There was a tentative finding against Global Marine at

99

close a look, had been towed from Redwood City to the semi-deserted Isthmus Cove of Santa Catalina Island, and there awaited the arrival of the *Explorer*.

The sight of these two strange vessels was to become somewhat common in the following months. Records indicate the barge visited the cove a total of five times. The ship, which wasn't needed for *HMB-1*'s first shakedown, made four trips to the sandy-bottomed inlet.

Eyewitness accounts of the manoeuvres are available. First, the barge would slowly begin to sink into the clear water. This process took some time, usually several hours. Then, finally, the huge metal contrivance would vanish beneath the surface, leaving only a few bubbles to mark its place. More time would pass, with no surface activity whatsoever, during which the barge was actually sinking lower and lower. When the *HMB-1* was about a hundred feet down, the *Hughes Glomar Explorer* would move into a precise position over it and, using its station-keeping capability, would hover motionless in the water.

To viewers on shore or in a boat some distance away, nothing would seem to happen, except the entrance to the small cove would be closed off by service craft and provisions would be taken to monitor the opening so as to stop the entrance of underwater surveillance devices.

Inside the ship, however, there was plenty of action. The vast Moon Pool had been allowed to fill with water, and its two doors, actually the 'bottom' of the ship, had been opened.

Next, the two huge docking legs, which when retracted form the triangular structures seen amidships on the vessel, were engaged and slowly lowered into the water. These legs, similar in design to the retractable supports used on some off-shore oil drilling rigs, have frequently been misidentified as nothing more than camouflage on the superstructure. *Parade* magazine, for example, published a photo of the ship in its May 11, 1975, issue, carrying a caption indicating the two triangulated structures were tacked into place to confuse Soviet observers.

These supports perform a vital function: they are the major load-bearing members during the undersea transfer of the weight of the subsea machinery from the barge to the lift pipe string. As the legs descend, the roof of the barge rolls back on order from the ship's computerized command centre.

During this phase, the position of the vessel is constantly being shifted, by minute amounts, to insure proper contact of the docking legs to the two huge pins projecting from the ends of the strongback control. The claw, inert and still, rests upright on the bottom of the steel barge.

At about a hundred feet down, the motions and turbulence of the surface are greatly reduced, and the pickup is made with uncanny ease. Slowly, the ends of each of the docking legs, now fully extended, begin to move towards each other through the water, tilting, like a pair of giant chopsticks, until they touch the docking pins. Once these pins engage the holes in the ends of the legs, the movement stops and contact is electronically affirmed in the master control area. Divers are available and may be used, if necessary, to assist in making this connection and in completing the other steps involved in the hookup.

Once the link is made, the barge is allowed to sink lower, leaving the claw and its bridlelike strongback free. Then, driven by their electric motors, the docking legs begin to retract, lifting the huge weight upward. This retraction continues until the entire machine is pulled up and into the open Moon Pool.

The whole underwater portion of the operation is observed on television receivers in the main control centre.

Once the claw is securely aboard, the docking legs are locked into position, and the multi-ton grapple is held suspended above the bottom of the ship. Then two things happen at once. The ship closes its massive underwater doors and begins to pump water out of the Moon Pool. At the same time, the top rolls closed on the barge, and air, forced from the surface, is vented in to replace the water ballast.

The ship, claw inside, sails away, and the barge, slowly and ponderously, rises again, in a spout of air, bubbles and foamy water. The waiting towboats return the *HMB-1* to its base where it remains until it is needed to take back its former load.

Within an hour of acquiring the claw and its controls, the entire Moon Pool is pumped free of water, and the machinery hangs suspended in mid-air from the two pins.

Light from batteries of lamps located along a catwalk high above the floor brilliantly illuminates the fascinating scene inside.

Men, suspended by ropes and working in harness, swing freely about this strange playground, carrying tools and wrenches as they work to link the strongback, which will carry the claw, to the pipe string. Others, with different-coloured hard hats, move about making necessary electrical connections. And still more are involved in joining hydraulic lines to the ship's system, so they will be able to manoeuvre the huge grapple when it is fully deployed and in place.

The one requirement of this operation is precision. A loose fitting or a careless electrical junction, so easy to correct now, will become an impossible problem three miles below the surface. So, swinging in their harnesses far above the metal floor of the ship, the men work with serious concentration.

They also work almost in silence, calling only to be raised or lowered as a position change becomes necessary. An occasional voice will sound in a request for a new tool, but everyone involved is giving his utmost to the job. Radio communication between the men cuts down the number of called-out requests, adding to the quiet of the room.

The number of connections is seemingly endless.

Wiring is needed for the acoustical sounders on the strongback used to generate the sonic waves necessary for creating undersea pictures. Then come the sonar devices, the various strain and depth gauges, and the hydraulic lockups for the main and slave controls. The 'plumbing' will be subjected to almost bursting pressures down deep, and there is no acceptable condition other than perfect.

Hours pass, and more. Connections are made, inspected and made again. Finally, everything is in readiness.

The giant derrick, high above the Moon Pool, positions the first section of pipe and lowers it slowly down. The connection with the strongback, made through a joint called a 'Dutchman,' is complete, and the ship is ready to begin lowering the claw. Or, with the docking legs locked into place holding the load, to set sail for the recovery area. This manoeuvre was difficult, at best, but the crew performed admirably, and after only one hookup, took the grapple aboard and headed for the salvage site. The worst was behind them. Hours of toil, hardship and the danger always inherent when dealing with huge masses of metal had gone into getting under way. The voyage itself was almost relaxing.

Travelling at her service speed of about 10 knots, the ship made good time across the rolling water. About 250 nautical miles per day were chalked up in her log, eating away at the 3,000-odd miles which separated her from the operations site. It took a little over 12 days to make the voyage, and, using the satellite location information confirmed by *Mizar* years before, they were guided into the recovery area without incident. But they were closely followed.

Several sightings of the Soviet trawler-type vessels had been made and several contacts reported on the over-the-horizon radar. Normal radar reception is limited to line of sight, but recent developments have provided for a beam which 'bends,' allowing for some contacts which otherwise would be out of range. Other surveillance was in effect, too, from Soviet satellites similar to our TIROS weather units, but modified to produce better pictures of aciivity at sea level.

Ignoring the audience, the *Explorer* crew located its precise position. Referring to the computer printouts and specially marked charts, they were satisfied all was well in the navigation department.

A brief bottom scan was the next order of business. Deep down in the sea, there are no eddies or currents. The storms passing over the surface miles above amount to nothing in the isolated, still depths. Blackness and silence are the rulers of this domain, insulated from the turbulence of the air ocean by endless amounts of water.

There was no reason to suspect the pieces of the broken hulk had moved from the specific locations provided by *USS Mizar*, but the exact positioning of the wreckage in relationship to the recovery vessel was critical.

For the next few days, *Explorer* cruised to and fro across an area limited by the information being channelled to the surface from various towed arrays of sonar, electromagnetic detection devices and the equipment required to produce acoustical pictures on the television-type screens in the main control area. The resolution of the pictures was said to be sufficient to discern individual welded seams and other details of the sub's construction.

Finally, satisfied with the collected data, the group of experts responsible for the recovery conferred and decided on the spot for the first attempt.

It was now time to deploy the Automatic Station Keeping System (ASK). The task of ASK is to keep the ship in a selected spot during the raising and lowering of the pipe lift string. The system is composed of several elements, and its deployment, although complicated in description, is relatively simple in practice.

The first action is to put out a buoy, equipped with electronic sensing devices and a sending unit, to make a communications link with the mother ship. This buoy is used to measure and monitor wave heights, and will notify the vessel if there is an abnormally great wall of water rushing down upon her. It is also used to determine if the operations may continue during periods of high wave and swell activity.

The sea heights are critical to the operation of the vessel, as are wind and a variety of other factors. In reality, a rather narrow 'window' in a wall of natural forces limits the actual seabed operations.

Maximum heave compensation (heave is the movement of a ship up and then down again as the wave rolls under it) is limited to plus or minus 6 feet. This means operations can continue in an 8-foot irregular sea, superimposed on a 12-foot, 12-second swell, at a water temperature of 45 degrees Fahrenheit.

Other maximum movements of the vessel are for roll, plus or minus $7\frac{1}{4}$ degrees over a 15-second period; and pitch, plus or minus 4 degrees over $7\frac{1}{2}$ seconds. Ideally, actual movements of the ship should be less than these parameters, and operations on the bottom must be suspended if sea states or ship movements are likely to exceed the above limits during a 36-hour period.

To be protected against unforeseen changes, there were on-board installations of the finest available weather equipment, including direct computer printouts from a teletype weather machine. On-going evaluations of both weather and sea conditions are a mandatory part of the vessel's operation.

If the round, orange and yellow wave-rider buoy indicates satisfactory swell-wave height, and the meteorologist feels the weather will be steady, the second phase of setting up the ASK system is commenced.

In order to function, the system measures vessel position in relation to a selected spot on the bottom, then constantly accepts data on wind speed and direction, ship heading, wave and swell condition, pitch, roll and several other factors. This information is processed, and automatic commands are given to the ship's thrusters and propellers to act against these combined forces, thus maintaining the vessel stationary in the water.

The thrusters are another uncommon feature of *Explorer*. Three of these 'water jets' are located along the lower side of the ship at the extreme end of the bow and two more are positioned at the stern. Each unit is placed so as to exert maximum leverage on the ship to move it sideways in the water. Each of these thrusters is capable of producing 40,000 pounds of force and, under extreme conditions, to deliver 44,000 pounds for limited periods. The thrusters work by pulling water in, then thrusting it out at very high rates of speed through their specially designed tubes.

With the wave rider indicating safe sea heights, and all power systems on 'go,' the next step is the deployment of the hardware for the first of the two systems to specify the station the vessel will hold until further notice.

The Short Baseline System (SBS) uses one beacon, lowered directly onto the ocean bottom, and four hydrophones, mounted on the ship's hull. Any three of these hydrophones will allow the SBS to function accurately. A backup vertical reference unit (two are installed, but only one is necessary) is another example of the redundant equipment included to ensure safety. The vertical reference units feed information to the ship's computer concerning the vessel's roll and pitch, and this is combined with data from the Bendix anemometers which sense wind gusts before they have time to act on the ship, allowing the computer to anticipate the need for thrust or propeller power. This action before the fact reduces the power required, as well as minimizing the margin of error. All these units, along with the computer, are also coupled to a pair of navigational gyro systems. One of these, a Sperry Mark 37 gyro compass, modified for this installation, monitors the ship's heading at all times and plays this data into the total programme.

Once the SBS beacon is on the bottom and sending, the

ship may then begin to deploy the far more accurate and sensitive Long Baseline System (LBS).

The LBS is the primary means for holding position, and consists of four transponders positioned in a huge square on the sea floor. On board the vessel, additional transponders constantly inquire for position data from those fixed on the bottom and, by determining the slant range of each diagonal of the square, derive a computer plot of the movement from the desired centre point. The total time required for the deployment of this system is considerable, even with a trained crew.

First, the various sending units must be lowered into place. This alone is a complicated manoeuvre. The ship lets down the first of the LBS transponder rings, then proceeds due north at the highest practical speed for a distance equal to 70 per cent of the depth of the water. Then it stops while the computer collects and analyses a second set of data. Three more starts and stops, each on a specified heading to a predetermined percentage of the water's depth are necessary for the deployment of the final transponders.

Then the calibration of the system is done by plotting fixes from the centre point to each of the now-established corners of the grid.

Once full operation of the system is confirmed by the technician in charge, the vessel is considered to have achieved station and may now maintain position within a 25- to 30-foot radius of the selected point.

Instructions in the ship's operating manual require more than 20 pages to detail this complex deployment, but, according to witnesses, it can be performed with some precision and, although time-consuming, is relatively simple to execute.

Each time the computer is fed a signal which it interprets as an energy sufficient to cause the ship to leave station, it activates the appropriate thruster or propeller, and applies a counter force, to remain in place. Since all the motors driving the props and thruster jets are operated on electricity, developed by diesel generators, there is no throb of engines, then silence, then a throb again. The power is applied smoothly in anticipation of the need, and most of the time those on board are unaware of the ongoing movements in the water.

Once station is attained, the checkout of the pipe lifting system and confirmation of the free working of the gimbals and other mechanisms which go to make up the stable working platform are the next goals.

The supported work area, located high above the open Moon Pool and topped by the towering derrick, is another of the ship's special systems.

As the vessel rolls, the gimbal mounts of this massive structure, which is taller than a three-storey building, allow it to rotate in the opposite direction, thus remaining flat and parallel to the surface of the water at all times. Additional dampening is provided for heave compensation, and the entire structure actually moves up and down, levelling the effects of the waves as they alter the water depth under the hull. A glass of liquid, full to the brim, placed on the surface of the platform will not spill.

Everything is now in readiness for the descent activity.

The claw and its strongback control have been attached to the first length of the lift pipe string. The exact positions of the pieces of the sub on the bottom, 16,500 feet below, have been clearly established and the decision made as to which broken part is to be brought up first.

The Long and Short Baseline Systems have been fully deployed, and the wave-height sensor, along with all weather gear, is feeding a steady stream of information into the station-keeping computer.

Finally, the Heavy Lift System (HLS), as well as the gimballed tower, has been checked and is ready for service.

All the endless preparation work is complete, and there is a real tension in the air, which breaks only when the final order is given to start forming the string.

The Moon Pool is flooded and the docking doors are fully opened.

The ship carries 600 lengths of 30-foot pipe, joined to form 60-foot segments of the string. Each 60-foot length is as strong as a cannon barrel and has met test after test for quality and manufacturing perfection. The weight of each length of the lift string varies but most fall about 40,000 pounds, roughly the same as a big Greyhound Scenic Cruiser bus.

Since the outside diameters of the pipe vary in thickness from 12.75 inches to 16.5 inches, the different-sized sections are colour-coded, red, white, blue, yellow, green or beige and the string will taper as it goes deeper.

The internal diameter of this multi-hued maypole is constant at 6 inches, allowing for a variation in the wall thickness of the lengths from 6.75 inches to 9.5 inches. About the same as a large field-artillery cannon.

Each piece of pipe has a slotted bulge at its ends and is tipped with a rubber O-ring and standard threads. When the threaded ends of two sections are screwed together, the rubber ring forms a seal and prevents accidental damage to the threads. The slots provide a locking grip for the automatic gripper which twists the pipes to thread or form the joint. The bulge is the grip point for the powered forks of the Heavy Lift System.

Men, working in slings suspended above the water in the now-full Moon Pool, make the necessary cable connections to the outside of the pipe. Their moves are coordinated to those of a second team on the deck above who are handling reels of cable and flexible hydraulic hose in readiness for including them in the soon-to-be constructed lift string.

Some of these connections will feed pictures of the work 3 miles below onto TV screens with resolution as good or better than the shots relayed from the moon during the manned missions. There is a lot of contrast, due to technical problems and the use of sound waves to 'light' the absolute blackness of the deep ocean, but because of the direct cable feed, there is no interference and the visual presentations are very clear. A total of 16 underwater TV cameras were on board, with 4 located just below the surface of the water on the ship itself.

Once the first pipe hookup is made, and while the necessary cables and plumbing are being deployed, the load of the claw is taken by the Heavy Lift System, and the 'parking brake' is set. This brake is a major innovation and a vital safety device. In case the ship is confronted with weather too severe for the ASK system to function, the load must not remain in contact with the sea bottom. Obviously, with the ship drifting more than the permissible 10 to 20 feet, the entire claw end, with whatever it is holding, would be bumping along the bed of the ocean, causing tremendous forces at the other end of the 16,500-foot link-up. According to the cautions stressed in the operating manuals, this situation would result in the complete destruction of the ship. When confronted with wave, wind, swell combinations beyond the limits of the system, the load is simply raised a thousand or so feet up, and suspended in place by the parking brake. The ship, thus supplied with a keel weighing millions of pounds and reaching far into the depths, actually becomes more stable.

Once the load weight is transferred from the docking legs, and they are retracted out of the way, it hangs suspended from the primary pipe length, held by the brake. At this point, the first sections are ready to be connected into the string.

The action is continuous, computer controlled and fully automated.

Men wearing intercom headsets direct the action from several positions. Two or three are on the main stabilized platform, while others man the cranes placed at each corner of the Moon Pool opening on the main deck. And still more are down below, where the multi-hued pipe stands are securely racked to prevent their rolling about as the ship moves. Additional technical staff maintains watch on the computers, hydraulic pump pressures and other critical equipment. In normal use, every action is recorded on tape for later review and study.

The crane operator starts the actual string building process, by calling below for a hookup. Men in hard hats move in, sling the crane's lifting cable to the first pipe length and then give the signal for the massive piece of machined steel to be lifted away. With one of the four working cranes taking the load, the pipe is pulled from its place in the rack and onto a two-piston device called the 'elevator.'

Once the section is in position, the crane hookup is released, and, while it swings back to pick another length from the rack, the elevator lifts the first piece straight up and out into the bright sunlight of the windswept main deck. A huge mechanical arm, moving with deliberate slowness, transfers the pipe from the elevator in a single motion and rolls it onto the 'sled' towering over the workmen standing nearby.

When the electronic control readings indicate the pipe is securely in place, the sled, hydraulically powered, starts its way up a steeply inclined ramp towards the second hookup point at the top of the derrick, high over the stabilized platform below. The ramp, with automatic controls to regulate its angle of ascent, is a huge triangular construction of steel, jutting from the derrick in a special position just above the stabilized work platform.

After a short but noisy journey, the pipe reaches the end of the sled track, and the sled is stopped just long enough for a cable connection to be made from the very top of the derrick to the swollen, bulged end of the pipe length. Then, with a coughing and revving of diesel engines, the piece is pulled free of the sled and upward towards the derrick drawworks.

Once the pipe is free, the sled descends, to be loaded again by a second, then a third and, finally, less than two days later, the 300th length.

The first piece of the string, which is now suspended from the very top of the derrick, is lowered until its end is in a mating position with the pipe sticking up from the end of the parking brake below, and as soon as they are touching, they are aligned and torque is applied to make the joint. Now, the load is taken up by the system, the parking brake released and the first 60 feet of depth is achieved.

The explanation takes almost longer than the action, for everything moves with a continuous, smooth precision, and a new length is added to the string each ten minutes.

The decks are awash with the sounds of engines, the clanking of steel on steel and the low voices of men talking into headsets and monitoring each part of the operation.

As the coloured sections are brought from below, it may become necessary to switch from the port to the starboard or the bow to the stern cranes, but the steel shafts continue to come up into the daylight, seemingly without human aid or assistance.

The process continues around the clock. In the early morning sunlight, the white of the ship and the bright industrial yellow of the triangulated sled ramp are dim outlines. By noon, the cobalt blue overhead is unbroken, and the sun beats mercilessly down until even the deck plates are too hot for contact with bare skin. As the afternoon lengthens, great shadows cross and recross the steel superstructure and the roaring, banging, clanging continues unabated. The smell of fuel and hydraulic oil is carried on the hot breeze. As night begins to fall, the scene takes on the air of a seafarer's hell. Bright lights, mounted everywhere, suddenly spring to life, making white pools of incandescent brilliance. The action started 12 hours before continues as the second crew takes over.

Finally, blackness falls, and the ship is a strange point of blinding light in the midst of a rolling, dark, and empty sea. But the pace remains constant. A length is tilted from

the rack onto the elevator, it is lifted, then rolled onto the sled, and it makes its journey upwards.

The colour of the pipe has changed, and the heavier lengths are now being moved with the same precision as the lighter first units.

On a deck, a cigarette glows brilliant red from a deep shadow, and a man materializes as he steps into the pool of light. Coffee as black as the night is passed around during a brief break, and the first rays of dawn appear before the work crews are changed again.

The metallic marathon continues. Hour after hour, the pipe is lowered, threaded into the growing string and lowered again. The mighty piston-driven arms grip the ever-lengthening string tightly, move downward through the space under the stabilized platform, stop, and pass the load to a second pair of arms. Then, rising again in perfect, mechanical time, they come back and seize the next pipe section.

We now arrive at a major point of difference with every published account of the Jennifer Project.

According to the manual of operation for the *Hughes Glomar Explorer*, and statements in a technical paper presented by a Global Marine engineer, the total string of pipe could be deployed to a depth of 16,500 feet in a matter of 45 to 48 hours or 3 to 4 crew shifts.

This is a rate of more than 340 feet per hour, every hour, around the clock. Providing there were no major malfunctions, this is a rate of deployment more than 20 times that stated in other reports. The rate question is important because of the length of time the ship is known to have been on station, and because of the later CIA-inspired 'whole sub' story.

Actually, *Explorer* was on site long enough to have gone down and brought back objects more than five times. Possibly as many as seven round trips could have been made, depending upon the unloading time and the nature of the cargo brought up on each trip.

Here, then, is another major discrepancy between the

facts of the vessel's capabilities, as documented in the ship's training and operations manuals, and the story presented by the CIA.

The eyewitness accounts of the on-site recovery, which provided the information for the descriptive passages above, give a very clear picture of the collection sequences. Those same accounts reveal an inventory of the actual items found in the broken hulk of the submarine, which also differs from the 'official' version.

Each of the men involved in the mission was given a thorough security check. Each was required to sign a security agreement covering his future conduct as far as openly discussing the mission. But some of these men have talked. Reports have been carried in *The Los Angeles Times* and in a few other newspapers.

The additional information revealed for the first time in this book is accurate. Yet no confidences were violated in its collection.

How the information was obtained is simple. The principles of good intelligence gathering were followed to the letter. Every source was checked and rechecked. Small bits of seemingly random data were compiled and, when placed into the perspective of the whole, had new meaning. Much new eyewitness experience of the operation of the vessel has been added, then checked against other accounts to confirm accuracy.

The men who manned the *Hughes Glomar Explorer* are patriots in the finest sense of the word. They were going into the unknown. They would be called upon to handle and deal with dangerously contaminated radioactive materials, and they might be boarded at any moment by a hostile Soviet contingent. They are proud of their achievement and have reason.

11

Contact was made with the first portion of the broken sub during the evening of the fourth day after the start of the operation. A minor problem slowed the process in the early hours of the first morning, and a couple of corrections were made during the course of the day to bring the work up to speed.

From there on, everything went smoothly. Even the meteorologist was pleased, because they were well within the weather window. The calm was holding, the up-and-down movement of the ship stayed under the design limit, and the ocean surface, where waves combined with swells, remained below the danger point.

Reality clearly now breaks away from the widely released CIA version which holds the sub to be intact. The *Hughes Glomar Explorer*, with the capacities listed in its own operations manual, could not have lifted the entire submarine.

The maximum payload weight on the string is stated to be 8,500,000 pounds at 17,000-foot depths. This is a total of 4,250 tons.

The hydraulically powered grappling machine, or claw, along with its small thrusters for manoeuvring when in place on the bottom, weighed, according to recently published figures, about 2,130 tons, in air. When this poundage is added to the combined weights of the electronic and hydraulic cables (3 miles of them), the connection bridle and the strongback, a total of slightly less than 6,500,000 pounds (3,250 tons) is achieved.

Jane's Fighting Ships, the recognized military reference work on vessel sizes, crews and armaments, gives the weight of the standard 'Golf-'class submarine as 2,350 tons, or 4,700,000 pounds. Correcting this figure for loss of nonmetallic items and the buoyancy of the water, the sub on the bottom, if it had been intact, would have weighed about 1,700 tons.

Added together, the total payload, based on lifting the sub whole, would have been not less than 4,900 tons.

The above calculation may be somewhat complex, but the net result is simple. The ship's lifting capacity was 450 tons short of being capable of picking up the sunken sub in one piece. And this allows no margin of overlift for safety, in a field where 50% margins of added capacity are normal and prudent.

Global Marine has published information which could be interpreted to indicate a capability of passing air down through the centre of the lift pipe string, which was normally filled with sea water and used as an hydraulic source to power the grapple. This air bouyancy system, it is claimed, accounts for a portion of the descrepancy. But any such bouyancy effect would be more than offset by the effects of suction between the sunken hulk and the ooze and mire of the bottom.

The whole subject of lift capacity and weight has been reported in many versions. *The Washington Post* gave the 'lifting capacity' of the *HMB-1* barge as 800 tons, when it has, of course, no lift capacity at all. And *The New York Times* used the same 800-ton figure for the capacity of the derrick. *Time* printed a diagram indicating the recovery device was composed of cables, and also reported a gross weight for the lift pipe string of 400,000 pounds. *Newsweek* offered a lift-system capacity of 12,000 pounds.

Part of everyone's problem is the immense size of

the equipment used on the job. Its capabilities defy reason.

Another difficulty is the variety of published figures emanating from Global Marine. This last confusion, however, is undoubtedly caused by a legal restraint on revealing the facts of the mission, combined with a natural desire to find a commercial outlet for their superior technology.

Weights aside, another excellent indicator of what the mission planners expected to find is the dimensions of the Moon Pool.

The *Hughes Glomar Explorer* was a ship designed from scratch for the performance of a single mission. Even though it might find later uses, the various recovery facilities, such as the Moon Pool, were predicated on the size of the components they would bring up from below. *Jane's* reports a 320-foot length for the 'Golf'-class submarine. The Moon Pool is 199 feet long.

There is also no question both the CIA and the Navy, from their excellent reconnaissance of the site, knew exactly what lengths the sub had broken into. Obviously, they were expecting to recover pieces less than 200 feet in length. It is foolish to assume they built a boat and then hauled up more than they could possibly handle.

The width of the Moon Pool is another matter. *Jane's* gives the width of the 'G'-class sub as 22 feet. The well, at 74 feet, is more than enough to house two sections of the vessel at one time.

The combination of the two items, insufficient lifting power and too little room in the well, is a practical rebuttal to the 'whole sub' story.

Another approach to the question could be: Is it possible for *Explorer* to have been designed to lift such a weight?

The increase in lifting power over *Alcoa Seaprobe*, the only other deep-sea recovery vessel at the time of *Explorer*'s launch, would be an advance of at least two orders of magnitude over the then state of the art. A pretty big jump, considering there had been no major breakthroughs in metallurgy providing new and stronger building materials.

George G. Scholley, president of Alcoa Marine Corporation, said flatly when questioned, 'There is no way on God's green earth they could have lifted the whole submarine up.'

In summary, then, we have these facts:

The *Hughes Glomar Explorer* was not designed to lift or contain an entire 'Golf'-class sub. There was no reason for such design.

In every reported instance of a sub sinking, the wreck has broken into at least three parts. This is true of *Thresher*, *Scorpion* and another Soviet vessel. To compound this, in the case of the sinking of the 'G'-class boat, there was a series of explosions on board which ruptured the hull sufficiently to have caused the sinking in the first place.

According to published quotes, even the experienced Captain Walker of the Office of the Navy's Oceanographer registered surprise at the CIA's claim.

Finally, we have one other item of proof: the testimony of individuals who were present at the time of the recovery.

The question of why the CIA chose to release a sham story will be covered in detail. But, first, here is a never-before-published account of the salvage effort.

First contact was made towards the end of the fourth working shift. The minor problems which stalled the operations temporarily during the first 12-hour run were cleared up, and the crews averaged well over 350 feet per hour.

Conditions were ideal. Once down to the correct depth, the sonar, acoustical devices and television cameras were used to study the position of the piece and determine the best grapple. Then, using hydraulic force and the built-in thrusters to turn the claw, contact was made and the jaws closed.

Coming up took a little longer, due to the need for careful handling of the captured piece, but was basically a reverse of the earlier process. The lifting yokes on the Heavy Lift System (HLS) gripped the pipe at the specially formed shoulders, and lifted the last section to be screwed into place free of the water. While it was held, the second yoke took its hold at the now-exposed joint, and locked on to stabilize the string. The last joint to be made was the first to be screwed loose, and the section of pipe, now free, was lifted to the tip of the derrick, where it was manoeuvred in reverse out onto the sled, then back down the ramp to the waiting crane. Even as it was being replaced in its storage rack, the sled was making the return trip to collect another length.

Naturally, the power required to come back up was considerably more than needed to go down. In addition to fighting gravity on a three-mile, straight-up pull, the added weight of the recovered part imposed strenuous loads on the equipment. 'You could hear the diesels huffin' and gruntin' all over the damn ship,' one source reported. 'And it was a noise that didn't stop, day or night.'

But the way up took very little longer than the original deployment, and four shifts later, the crushed and battered centre segment of the sub, with the shattered fragments of the front portion of the sail, was drawn up into the Moon Pool.

No chronology is available for the exact sequence of the removal of artifacts from the hulk. Even eyewitness accounts are hazy, because of the intense security clamped down on the operation: but developing a reliable overall picture is not too difficult.

First, sections of the hull plate had to be cut away to gain complete access to the interior of the vessel. Then, a systematic salvage operation was carried out with relative ease.

After a thorough monitoring for radioactive contamination, with precautions taken so as not to expose the workmen, the first segment of the hulk was sliced free and lifted onto the foredeck where the gantry crane could be used in speeding up the laying out of the various sections. The men had to work with extreme care, yet at top speed, so as to minimize exposure of the recovered sub to the eyes of the Russians, who were still snooping in the area.

The recovered portion, especially after being hacked apart, bore little resemblance to a submarine or any other kind of boat. From a distance, it must have looked like some kind of strange steel free-form sculpture.

In any case, examination of the recovered segment and the removal of items was going on while the next phase of the recovery effort started up again.

Explorer was moved to a second and then a third site. Each time, the involved process of establishing the station-keeping short and long base lines was executed. The buoy-type wave rider, with the electronics package on top, was deployed to measure the wave heights. The weather station on board established itself in the new location, and began feeding the ASK system the latest wind information from the pair of anemometers. The computer also would start to take input from the gyro compass, to maintain the ship's heading during the operation.

Finally, everything would be in readiness and the bottom scanning effort would start anew. Then, with the layout established, the pipe would be lowered for the next contact.

The relocation and redeployment of the equipment must have appeared to be normal to the spying Russians. After all, in a mining operation, the ship would have been expected to select a site, make a pass, collect as much of the available mineral deposits as possible, then relocate to repeat the process.

One Soviet ship, however, wanted a better view and began to move in closer and closer to the stationary *Explorer*. The pipe crew on the decks could see themselves being watched and photographed by the Russians, who were using large telephoto lenses.

The story goes that almost at the same instant, and without a single spoken command, the men on the platform raised their right hands, middle finger ended, in the international sign of derision or friendship. This 'bird' shooting seemed to have produced an effect, because the Soviet ship opened its distance and never repeated its in-close performance.

At another time, a different group on deck gathered on the large helicopter pad at the stern of the ship and, after dropping their trousers, 'mooned' the astonished Russians.

The actual order of what was recovered is unimportant. Only the final inventory of items matters. The metallurgists got their steel plate and weld samples and had a field day determining the origin of the ore, the quality of the materials, the design depth of the boat and a thousand other things.

According to Representative Joseph P. Addabbo, Democrat of New York, who took part in CIA chief William E. Colby's off-the-record briefings, Colby himself, not withstanding his public denials, told the group two nuclear torpedoes had been a part of the recovered materials.

There is reason to believe even more was found. One eyewitness told of how the entire salvage operation was severely hampered by nuclear contamination from the recovered objects. All workers on board wore radiation detectors attached to their hard hats.

According to another reliable source, a portion of the salvage crew's special schooling had been spent working in 'space suits' to protect themselves from radioactive materials. Despite the precautions, the informant himself received radiation burns and 'totally ruined a new pair of damn expensive boots.' The scintillation counter used to detect radioactivity 'went all the way to the peg' when he entered the decontamination area, and he had to 'shower myself for an hour and a half' to get rid of all traces.

Another report recounts the recovery of the body of a Soviet nuclear expert, along with his 'personal journal and two nuclear tipped torpedoes.' The missiles, normally housed in the forward part of the sail, must have been salvaged too and, even in their leaking states, undoubtedly provided the onboard experts with more than enough to keep them busy.

The bodies of several seamen were also brought up. Reports on the number range from a low of 7 to a high of 70 – a very wide spread.

The normal crew of a 'G'-class boat is a complement of 12 officers and 74 men, for a total of 86 persons. The remains of some of these unfortunate seamen were lost during the breaking up of the vessel. Others were totally crushed by the pressure of the water or by the explosion which caused the sinking in the first place.

Eyewitnesses agree on the recovery of between 50 and 60 bodies or parts of bodies. Their accounts also indicate the remains, after 6 years and a pressure of 7,000 pounds per square inch, were mostly in unrecognizable shape. However, artifacts such as clothing and personal effects were revealing and provided a good picture of the crew's composition and life style on board the sub.

Among the most valuable finds was the body of the previously mentioned nuclear specialist. A junior officer, he was identified from his 'dog tags,' after his body was discovered curled up in a narrow bunk. His diary was found nearby. What made this of special interest is the fact he had been one of the on-board nuclear weapons experts, and his journal covered every phase of his student training and subsequent sea operations. The diary, like other printed manuals, was in sad shape after its years of immersion, but salvage, through the use of high-vacuum drying techniques, restored the material to usability.

In a slightly more macabre vein, the physiologists and forensic medicine boys found the recovered remains of some interest. Since the depths of the sea are thought to be lifeless, decomposition of the bodies would have had to come from the bacteria carried by the individuals while they were alive. The post-mortem reports provided sufficient data for several papers and memos.

One of the most sombre events occurred when an official funeral, conducted in both English and Russian and following the procedures in the Soviet Navy's own book of ceremonies, was performed. A special contingent of government personnel was airlifted to the ship by helicopter, and the entire service took place in front of cameras and recording equipment, so a complete record, including the consignment of the bodies back to the depths, would be available.

A close CIA source, when questioned about why such a service had been held, reported there had been a lot of discussion on the matter, and the decision had been reached based on a concern for negative public opinion if the operation was ever blown and the recovery became public knowledge. No one wished to be thought of as callous, and the interment ceremony was designed to show proper respect for the fallen men.

The salvage of the code machine and the code books is apparently open for debate. An exclusive eyewitness reports 'at least I know for sure they got some kind of code books, because everybody was goin' half nuts over 'em.' The CIA has denied, in all its unofficial releases, any success in this area.

Again, the weight of fact seems to lie with the eyewitness. It is unlikely code devices would have been overlooked or missed. Since either a book or a machine would have been kept under tight security, probably even in a safe of some kind, it is hard to believe they were swept overboard during the sinking. Subsequent comments by various congressmen seem to indicate code equipment was among the salvaged items.

Then there is the question of the Ship's Internal Guidance System (SIGS).

It is hard to assess the effect of immersing electronic printed circuits in pressurized salt water, but there can be little question the CIA, which experimented to find out what happens to paper documents printed with various inks, ran tests on other components long before the recovery effort was decided upon. The Navy also, from its own experience, would have an excellent backlog of this type of information.

An electronic engineer, speaking off the record, stated, 'A thing as complicated as a SINS [Ship's Internal Navigation System] probably wouldn't work. It wouldn't be able to carry a current. But let me examine it, take it apart so to speak, and we could build another one just like it. Or give a pretty good insight into its performance. Especially if we had access to our own design technology in the field.'

The SIN System, or any other complex electronic package such as the Ship's Internal Guidance System (SIGS), the basic sonar on board, a homing device for the torpedoes, or the launch and direction control for the recovered Serb-class missiles would be of enormous value. All this gear had to be on board the sub and in operating condition at the time of its disaster. It simply doesn't make sense to conclude these items were not recovered.

On one subject eyewitnesses and the unofficial CIA releases do agree: the retrieval of a vast array of papers and documents, including pinup pictures from several of the Soviet seamen's lockers.

It seems a safe area for concurrence, as there can be little doubt both our men and theirs are motivated by the same basic drives. It is also of little strategic import-ance to know men from the Kazakstan prefer their girl friends a little heavier bellied and meatier than do men from Omaha, Nebraska.

There is, then, a vast difference between the CIA's intentionally leaked version of the items recovered and the sum of the on-the-spot eyewitness and other reports.

The CIA, moreover, seems to be inconsistent in its stories.

When we add information obtained from published facts about the sunken sub's capacity and operating abilities to the later comments of elected officials who attended the closed CIA debriefing sessions, the balance loads in favour of the eyewitness accounts. The CIA is not telling all. And its withholding of information follows a pattern.

In the CIA unofficial-official version, nothing of value was obtained and the mission was almost a total bust. This is clearly not the case. A great many things were recovered and study of the items has provided information well worth the price of the operation.

It seems strange for the CIA to have leaked any kind of story at all. In the traditions of the intelligence business, it's just plain bad form to be caught in the middle of any clandestine operation. The only good job is the one kept secret. But bad as it is to be caught, it's a lot worse to end up red-faced and unsuccessful as well. And this is exactly the position in which the CIA has placed itself in relationship to the Jennifer Project. Not only does the CIA privately admit there was such an operation, it says over and over again it was a failure. In many ways, this is the strangest part of the entire affair.

Why did the CIA, even on an unofficial basis, admit to having been involved in the first place? The Navy, after all, had instigated the project and the episode could have been pushed off onto their plate with some ease.

Or, better still, and more in keeping with the practices of the spy service, why say anything at all? The CIA is well staffed with people who are experts at stonewalling attempts for information. If the press wants to speculate on the possibility of a secret operation, well and good; but there is no reason for official position-taking, even on a confidential, man-to-man level.

Yet this is exactly what happened.

Seemingly nervous, for the first time in recorded

memory, over the growing speculation about any project, Director of the CIA William Colby telephoned and personally visited the managing editors of several newspapers. First he wanted the story killed. Then, when this was deemed impossible, he violated standard practice and gave out a story, admitting there had been an operation. Next he claimed it had been a total disaster.

Notice the involvement of the Director himself, and not one of the literally hundreds of press-representative types employed by the agency. Nor was the job relegated to one of his upper echelon deputies. CIA visits to the press, to ask for cooperation, have occurred before; but seldom by the Director of 'The Company.' Certainly not by a Director who admits the action but claims failure.

The amount of effort placed behind the 'whole sub' story must have been immense, because the controversy carried over into late 1976. A stir was caused by an article in a December 1976 issue of *Time* magazine which stated the operation was a success. The story cited a 'high-ranking' naval officer as its source. This article was quickly followed by a Seymour Hersh rebuttal in *The New York Times* which once again reiterated the 'whole sub was recovered but a part was lost' theme.

In Hersh's account, the size of the Moon Pool, which he erroneously gives as 200 feet by 65 feet, is accounted for by a plan to have divers cut up the sub while it was being brought to the surface and then dock only the valuable centre section. It's difficult to imagine how this would have been accomplished while the wrecked hulk was in the grip of the claw. Engineers with whom this novel proposal has been discussed smiled in amusement at the concept. But in any case, the two stories, years after the event, indicate the weight given the subject in the first place.

Whatever power caused the CIA to react in this untypical and, for the CIA, slightly irrational fashion, had to be of major magnitude. It's almost as if some great force, working outside the normal frame of reference, produced massive response.

This is exactly what took place.

The story of how and why is the part of Project Jennifer which makes it even more difficult to decipher and more fascinating than most other intelligence operations. It provides a fitting end to the strangest, and certainly from the standpoint of information gained, most successful actions on record.

To place things into their proper slots, some background is necessary. It's interesting material, and although totally factual, it sounds almost like fiction. Where did the CIA come from? How was it created? Why? What is its major role? How is it controlled?

Once these questions are answered, the facts of the Jennifer Operation can be fitted into the framework, and the results are truly revealing.

12

Intelligence gathering in America goes back at least to
Nathan Hale, who, dressed as a Dutch schoolmaster (his
own real-life trade), penetrated the British lines on Long
Island in September 1776. Hale, captured with numerous
maps and notes concerning the deployment of British
troops and defences, was ordered hanged by Gen. Sir
William Howe, the British commander.

If Hale was America's first man out in the cold,
Benedict Arnold was her first 'Mickey.' A 'Mickey' is the
spy business term for an agent who 'walks in' and offers
the other side something of value. In Arnold's case, it
was the strategic fort at West Point. Sir Henry Clinton,
the British general to whom Arnold was to hand over
the keys, also used agents. But his man, John Andre, like
Hale, had the misfortune of getting caught while trying
to set up the deal (or 'complete the contract', as they say).

America's first use of tricky spy devices also goes back
to the same era. Silas Dean, a political agent from the U.S.
to France, used invisible ink to communicate with his
American contacts.

By the time the Civil War rolled around, America
had apparently learned enough about the value of such
activities to cause both the Union and Confederate sides
to field fairly well-organized intelligence operations.
Union Maj. Allan Pinkerton's group was astonishingly

complete, and their work proved to be very effective.

Basically, the government has always felt there was something a little shady about the whole spy business – all right for the military in times of war and all that, but during peaceful periods, quite out of the question. Which sums up most of the history of U.S. operations in this area until after World War II.

During a state of national emergency, the need for information becomes dire and the demand for making the right decision crucial. So the U.S. would engage in the craft of intelligence. But when the world situation eased, we relaxed and returned to our more honourable ways. Besides, information gathering costs money. Staffs and agents have to be paid.

The entire matter of acquiring intelligence was left, by and large, to the military, who, many civilians felt, were involved in a sort of dirty business anyway. The decision suited everyone, because the staffs of admirals and generals were well aware of the necessity of on-going information gathering. Col. Ralph H. Van Deman, considered by many the father of our modern military intelligence, was a moving force during World War I in establishing a continuing organization.

By 1918, both the Army and the Navy had intelligence branches and they maintained themselves, albeit sometimes in reduced form, during the period between the Armistice and the start of World War II. Most of the Army organizations were grouped under G-2, a term used to define information for use in field or combat situations and expanded to cover all military knowledge, CIC (Counter Intelligence Corps) which grew out of the Corps of Intelligence Police, the CID (Criminal Investigation Division) and others.

The Navy, always more elegantly organized then its land-based cousins, grouped its activity into one general area and called it the ONI (Office of Naval Intelligence), even though it had functions similar to G-2 and CIC in operation.

served as U.S. Secretary of State under Eisenhower, came from a family with a history of public service.

Both his grandfather, John W. Foster, and his uncle, Robert Lansing, served as Secretaries of State. There was a family tradition for the office.

While still in college, he was able to attend the second Hague Conference under the auspices of his grandfather and was thus exposed early to the rigours of international relations. Dulles entered the international law firm of Sullivan and Cromwell in 1911, and fifteen years later was the head of that organization, after having been made a partner in 1920.

A Republican by birth and inclination, he nonetheless was appointed by Democratic President Wilson to a position on the reparations committee established at the end of World War I to settle losses incurred during that conflict. Prior to this, he was legal counsel at the Versailles Conference which helped end the bitter struggle. Later, when the formation meetings of the United Nations were held at Dumbarton Oaks, near Washington, D.C., Dulles was a key figure in the development of the U.N. charter. He also served as a senior adviser during the U.N. conference in San Francisco.

In 1949, Thomas E. Dewey, the mustachioed two-time Republican hopeful who had lost to both FDR and Truman, appointed Dulles Senator from New York to fill an unexpired term. Shortly after this, in 1950, he was named as a consultant to the State Department and assigned the negotiation of the final peace treaty with Japan.

Dulles showed his brilliance in this task. In place of convening an international meeting, which might have caused phenomenal delays and assuredly would have produced compromise after compromise as the individual nations jockeyed for position, he travelled more than 125,000 miles to the various national capitals, where he personally conducted the negotiations on a face-to-face basis. The phrase 'globe-trotting diplomacy,' later applied to Henry Kissinger, was coined to describe Dulles' tireless activity.

Dewey's selection of Dulles to fill the remaining days of the Senate term was no accident. Dewey, along with other 'Eastern Establishment' movers and shakers in the Republican Party (Nixon has been named by some as being included in this group), felt it was time for the U.S. to viably enter the intelligence business on a big-time basis. One of their great hopes was John Foster's brother, Allen, who was an experienced, committed intelligence expert.

By appointing John Foster Dulles, Dewey gained both an able man for the government and a strong ally in the fight to establish an American intelligence organization.

Allen Dulles had benefited from an interesting career. He completed college only a few months before the outbreak of World War I and in the next few years worked his way around the world. He taught school in India and travelled widely in the Far East. By the time of America's entry into the world conflict in 1915, he had joined the diplomatic service, where he eventually became Chief of the Near East Division of the State Department. During his career, he was, in his own words, more an 'intelligence officer than a diplomat.'

He and his brother, John Foster, were close, having enjoyed a strong childhood relationship. When Allen left the State Department in 1926, he moved to his brother's law firm, where he stayed until he could again practise his true craft.

During World War II, Allen rose to a high position in the Office of Strategic Services. When the OSS was disbanded in 1945, there was a general ground swell of disappointment from the group of believers, and they increased their efforts, more convinced than ever of America's need for a powerful intelligence function.

Allen Dulles, backed by his brother's contacts and using all of his own as well, began a strong campaign to resurrect the defunct OSS in some form. Allen, Foster

Dulles, Dewey and others, felt the need to fight fire with fire.

In Europe, the Soviet use of the KGB, its spy arm, was having visible effects on the stability of the governments of several countries. It was apparent the United States would be unable to maintain its dominant world position without a first-rate intelligence capacity.

The result of their efforts was the creation in 1947 of the Central Intelligence Agency. Provided for as a part of the National Security Act, the agency was this country's first peace-time, civilian-controlled intelligence organization.

A year later, Harry Truman appointed Allen Dulles, William Jackson and Mathias Correa as a special three-man committee, charged with the development of a report on the effectiveness of the CIA and its relationship with other intelligence organs of the government. The report was submitted to Truman on his re-election, and later in 1950, Allen was called back to Washington by Gen. Walter Bedell Smith, then head of the CIA, to implement several of the ideas contained in the recommendation. Two years and a few months later, Allen Dulles was the Director of the CIA.

John Foster Dulles had a slightly shorter wait for an appointment to his calling. The victory of Truman over Dewey in 1948 came as a surprise to everyone, and, since Democratic Presidents don't normally have Republican Secretaries of State, four more years would have to pass before John Foster Dulles would gain his position. Finally, after the election of Dwight Eisenhower, he was sworn into office in January 1953. Shortly thereafter, Allen attained the CIA directorship.

John Foster Dulles was determined to lead public opinion instead of following it. The hardness of his line on communism is credited by many for checkmating the Soviet cold-war strategy. He also was responsible for an often misquoted remark in a magazine article he authored in January 1956. The line is indicative of his understanding of U.S./Soviet relationships of the time: 'The ability to get to the verge [of war] without getting into the war is the necessary art. ... If ... you are scared to go to the brink, you are lost.'

This espoused philosophy of brinkmanship played a key role in the direction CIA activities would take in the seven years John Foster Dulles was to hold office. His relationship with his brother, Allen, remained close. They thought alike on matters of international policy. Acting together, they forged a role for the CIA in the international arena.

John Foster wanted an effective arm which could be called upon to effect changes, by means of money or force, in problems influencing the policies of his State Department. Allen, writing in his book *The Craft of Intelligence*, says, 'He [his brother] became a convinced supporter of the work of the new Central Intelligence Agency.'

Slowly, as facts of recent history have shown, the CIA became a practical, working adjunct of the Department of State, and the main thrust of its efforts was dictated by the primary goal established by that department. Namely, the stopping of the communist threat before additional countries might fall under its stranglehold.

Both the Iranian affair concerning Mossadegh and the Chilean involvement over Allende have been widely reported and cried over, but the CIA is a Johnny-come-lately to the techniques pioneered and still used by the Soviet KGB. The recent clandestine involvement of the KGB in the 1976 Italian elections is a matter of record.

The CIA started at a disadvantage because of its lack of experience in the art of juggling force, money and influence, but it soon caught up. Because its leaders found themselves enrolled in a school with very high tuition, and very valuable lessons.

The agency, however, did not replace any of the military intelligence forces. The Army, Navy and, to a lesser extent, the Air Force continued to conduct widespread intelligence projects of their own design, specializing in nonstrategic activities with relatively immediate results.

Occasionally, because of intraservice problems or other difficulties, one of the military arms would approach the CIA for help. Project Jennifer is a perfect example. The concept of the programme was Navy, the preliminary reconnaissance was Navy and, to a great extent, the financing came from funds included in the Navy budget. The role of the CIA was one of execution.

But in the 1950's, The Company's basic purpose was to aid the Department of State with intelligence, information and opinions, and, when called upon, to take an aggressive part in the support of U.S. diplomatic policy. These activities included financing candidates in foreign elections (and, some say, selected candidates in our own elections as well), conducting clandestine operations for the purpose of removing individuals who were hostile to U.S. policies, and other 'more than information' involvements.

The formative years for the establishment of the role of the CIA were those during which John Foster Dulles was Secretary of State and Allen Dulles was the Director of the agency. State called the shots, and the CIA scored the hits.

For the most part, this work took place on foreign soil, but some recent revelations indicate there was also a fairly concerted 'internal U.S.A.' operation. It seems logical. If the CIA would go so far as to influence foreign elections so a candidate favourable to U.S. policy would win an election, there is no apparent reason the same thought process wouldn't also try to influence the selection of the makers of that policy.

Involvement in U.S. politics by members of the CIA had its roots in this period, but would take almost two decades to flower. CIA involvement in domestic activities would be discussed during the events leading to the first resignation of a U.S. President.

State Department control of the CIA underwent a drastic change when the Dulles combination was broken.

John Foster, ill with cancer, resigned on April 15, 1959, and died a little over a month later. Allen, who served until late in 1961, continued cooperation between the two departments. But a new President, this time a Democrat, intervened after one dreadful occurrence, and the relationship between State and the CIA was temporarily altered.

Shortly after his election, during a special briefing, President John F. Kennedy was presented the Bay of Pigs project as an accomplished fact. The entire operation, designed to end Fidel Castro's rule of Cuba, had been developed over a period of years, behind President Dwight Eisenhower's back. However, then Vice President Richard Nixon, as head of one of the National Security Council's supervisory subcommittees, called the '54/12 Group,' had complete knowledge of the plan almost from the time of its inception.

In addition to the Bay of Pigs, and this is something Kennedy may or may not have known, the CIA also developed and carried out a well-documented series of assassination attempts against Castro. All these tries failed – some from poor execution, and others by peculiar happenstances of fate – but the effect they had on the Cuban attitude towards the U.S. is still being felt.

It is clear if Nixon had been elected in 1960, the Bay of Pigs project would have received far greater support. As it happened, the whole affair fell in a shambles when CIA officials reportedly requested Kennedy to use U.S. Air Force planes in a desperate last-minute counter-strike to allow the defeated and demoralized invading group time to reorganize. Kennedy, aware of the threat posed by Soviet intervention on Castro's side, refused, and the operation ground to a bloody halt. The aftermath was terrible, both for the still living members of the invading army and the CIA.

Kennedy felt victimized by the agency. The operation had been forced on him, and suddenly he was stuck with the full responsibility. He was supposed to have expressed his feelings to one of his aides, saying he would like to see the CIA 'splintered into a thousand pieces, and scattered to the winds.'

The failure of the Bay of Pigs project, the largest the CIA had attempted, marked the end of Allen Dulles as Director.

John McCone, an able Wall Street attorney, was named as Dulles' successor, and came into office needing to rely on the experienced individuals who staffed The Company. Richard Helms, who had been trained in agency management by Dulles, proved helpful and was allowed to maintain his jurisdiction over the CIA 'dirty tricks' division. The assassination attempts on Castro were continued for the next few years, without recorded Presidential sanction.

A period of interregnum occurred when Kennedy was assassinated.

Lyndon B. Johnson, who took charge immediately on attaining the Presidency, was a man of great personal determination. His knowledge of national politics and the operation of the legislative machinery in both Houses was unsurpassed, but he was less experienced in dealing with foreign policy, and difficulties almost immediately confronted him.

By 1964, Johnson was totally involved in the Vietnam situation, which was so far advanced it was taking all available manpower. The Vietnam War, along with violence caused by internal dissidence at home, gave the CIA a full plate of action.

President Johnson was leery of the CIA on two counts. First, because he'd had a ringside seat during the Bay of Pigs operation and learned a lesson from Kennedy's discomforting situation. Second, he was from the old school and oriented away from clandestine machinations.

The CIA, in recognition of Johnson's deep and abiding knowledge of the interworkings of government, laid off almost all their domestic support of politicians.

Richard McGarrah Helms was 53 years old when he gained the directorship and was the first, if we discount Allen Dulles, professional intelligence official to occupy the position. His career had begun in World War II and he was an 'old boy' in that he had served in the OSS and had been with the CIA since its inception. To some extent, he inherited a sinking ship.

Vice Admiral William F. Raborn, his predecessor, who replaced John McCone during the Johnson Administration, had been an outsider to everyone in the intelligence business, and morale was low. Worse, the agency itself, with no strong friend in either President Johnson or the Secretary of State, had come under increasing fire by Congress and assorted other agencies of the government.

Helms, a tall, lean, even-tempered man with a strong sense of humour, had his work cut out for him. The fractionation which had taken place in the ranks of The Company is said to have been his main difficulty. According to some speculation, a portion of the CIA had set up its own secret currency and banking empire, and had made millions of dollars in profits by using the agency's very advanced information on the market, currency fluctuations and other financial matters to invest portions of funds allotted for operations.

Select members of The Company were in an admirable position to have done exactly this. No one is certain to this day about the total amount of monies allotted in the organization, and major portions of CIA funds, intended for secret payoffs and other undercover work, were available to many individuals on an almost 'no question' basis. This money, coupled with specific intelligence, could well have been used for investment .This may have made the agency, and perhaps some operators, extremely wealthy. No report has ever been made public on this speculative problem, but there is reason to believe it is one which confronted Helms soon after taking office.

A second, more ticklish, difficulty was the emergence of the 'at home' gang, who wanted a more active role in the formation of foreign policy through influencing the outcome of selected U.S. elections.

Helms was able to at least limit both of these offshoot activities.

His days, however, as Director were numbered by Johnson's refusal to run for re-election. And it was no surprise when he was replaced, during Richard Nixon's first term, by James Schlesinger, a proven member of the new President's team.

Nixon's relationship with the CIA is interesting. He appears, like his adviser, Henry Kissinger, to have been fascinated with the clandestine side of the intelligence trade. He had been a formative force in the creation of the agency, aligning himself with Thomas Dewey and the Dulles brothers. But when he called upon the agency to ally itself with his Administration and carry out a series of domestic, ethically questionable acts, the CIA refused. When the agency still denied cooperation even after endless amounts of hot water had been poured on it, Nixon wrote it off. It was no longer the President's own, and the agency became fair game on Capitol Hill.

By June 27, 1970, the order of the CIA day became business as usual when Henry Kissinger, then a National Security Adviser, was one of the group approving the Chilean Operation. This action, eventually to cost millions of dollars, was a clandestine programme designed to prevent the election of Marxist Salvador Allende as President of Chile. It served notice that the CIA was once again to be the strong arm of the State Department.

The segment of the agency concerned with the election of individual politicians here at home also found itself in a climate supportive to its desires, and began to hold larger sway, leading the CIA into a role in American politics in no way authorized by the original founding directive.

Finally, in September 1973, William Egan Colby was named by Nixon to the directorship, and the agency once

again had a man who was a career intelligence officer. From the start, Colby was traditional in the execution of his role as director, and the agency once again came under the influence of the State Department.

Kissinger further tightened his control of the agency through his election to the half-secret 40 Committee, a kind of board of directors governing the nation's spying system. This body was very powerful in the intelligence community and was charged with making certain the CIA's projects were worth potential political risk.

For years, the group met on a weekly basis, but recent reports indicate the meetings occurred with less and less frequency under Kissinger's tenure as Secretary of State. In 1972, only one meeting was reported, and that single conference was apparently very informal, accepting reports about operations already set into motion by the President.

No meetings at all are recorded in the press in 1973 and 1974, but one report indicates some of the committee's work was carried out by telephone calls. *Newsweek* magazine, in 1974, called Kissinger the dominant member.

The 40 Committee's role in the approval of Project Jennifer, along with the tradition of the CIA's involvement, and sometimes solitary service to the Department of State, lies at the bottom of the behaviour of the CIA in regard to Jennifer's success.

Henry Kissinger's powerful influence on U.S. foreig policy began to manifest itself shortly before the re part of Operation Jennifer. The extent of his influence the operation itself is hard to assess, but there are amp reports to forge a clear connection between his attitu towards the CIA and the eventual denouncement of success of the project.

Since its formation, the CIA has made its share mistakes, as well as carried off a number of major co Its close, on-again, off-again involvement with Department of State has caused the agency to inv

itself time and time again in activities outside the scope of its originally intended mission.

But the organization has been effective. The efforts of the 18,000-odd people, who work with huge budgets, have delivered information which has proved crucial in the development of America's foreign policy and defence plans.

The real problem in the CIA lies in the fact it can stand no publicity. If a project is successful, then, by definition, it remains secret. If everything goes ideally well, the agency would never appear to have done anything at all.

The KGB, as do most of the other major foreign intelligence-gathering forces, receives special treatment from its own press. At least, when a project goes awry, it's never mentioned at all. In the United States, however, the CIA is news. And since the only time we hear of it is when something busts, it appears to have a relatively ineffective record.

President Truman once stated 95 per cent of the U.S.'s secret information had been published by newspapers and magazines. His argument was that newsmen should withhold certain information even when it had been made available to them. Our system seems to work pretty well, however, and no changes are immediately foreseeable. If anything, judging from the amount of intelligence we gather from other countries' news media, the trend seems to be more towards our style of reportage.

In the heat of a full press investigation, a certainty when a major fumble has occurred, people in public service tend to disassociate themselves from the agency. During one such period, spokesmen for the State Department tried to support the premise that CIA station chiefs were constantly taking action without the knowledge of our ambassadors. In other words, the State Department called the ambassadors' authority a 'polite fiction.' In the light of the relationship between the State Department and the agency and the known strength of our ambas-

sadorial staff, this stand received unofficial ridicule from members of Congress who knew better.

Congress itself sometimes makes major problems for the CIA. The agency is approached with a number of schemes – some good, some bad – by many branches of the government. A great part of this is due to its method of funding. Usually, and this is widely known in Washington, the CIA can find money when no one else can. If a Congressman gets behind a proposal, the agency is in a real bind. It often cannot reveal other activities under way which would render the new idea unfeasible, or at least redundant. Also it's hard to say 'no' when there is a very real risk of angering a powerful political figure. More than one unofficial report has circulated about other agencies taking on jobs originally proposed to the CIA and thus becoming, in a sense, rivals.

In many ways, then, it's impossible for people in power to be favourable towards a CIA operation. If they know about it, unless they are members of a tiny select circle, too many other people also know, and the project will soon be blown up as another CIA fiasco.

Henry Kissinger, to a degree, had the same difficulty. Obviously, if an opportunity existed for him to avoid public recognition of a failed project, he would be foolish not to take it. If the operation about to come into the limelight was one with potentially embarrassing overtones for the Soviets, it would be incompatible with the policies of detente which he forwarded.

His control over the CIA, while not perhaps absolute, was, during the period covered by the Jennifer Project, considerable. As Secretary of State, he had tradition behind him. As head of the National Security Council and a member of the 40 Committee, he was in a direct position to influence CIA actions. As confidant to the President and the friend of important Capitol Hill people, he could direct vast amounts of pressure and effort to the fulfilment of his ideas.

It is unreasonable to assume his role in the ending of

the Jennifer Project was totally passive. His involvement, along with the CIA's allegiance to the Department of State, provides an excellent explanation for the next events.

13

The *Hughes Glomar Explorer* remained on station at the recovery site for a total of 40 days, then set sail on August 12, 1974, towards the island of Maui in the state of Hawaii, 750 miles to the southeast.

The crew, relieved at not having been boarded by the Soviets, was still anxious to be in American waters, so they held their speed close to the maximum 10.5 knots, and arrived in the islands on August 16. But there was no immediate attempt at docking.

On board, the activity of the scientific group was continuing at a terrific pace. The amount of recovered material from the last section of the sub was still being analysed and discussed. A complete catalogue of all information gained was being prepared, by subject, before the group of experts left the vessel. Two more weeks would be required to wrap up this phase of the activity, and rather than remain on station even a day longer than necessary, continuing the very real risk of detection by the Soviets, it was decided to head for a home territory as soon as possible, and complete the work in friendly waters.

During the next 14 days, several news reports were filed about the ship, mostly commenting on its apparently listless and aimless cruising in the waters around Hawaii. One story from a man on board, never before published, stated the vessel was being used as a scenic cruiser and, while the scientific and engineering team worked, the lift pipe crew and the ship's complement went sight-seeing, and, when possible to do so without being seen, deep-sea fishing.

Finally, on the evening of August 30, agreement was reached on a plan to wrap up the balance of the work. The information was split into two components. The reports, a catalogue of recovered items and some sample material in need of further testing to complete the basic overview report stayed with the CIA scientific complement. The second component, which consisted of parts of the actual nuclear weapons, hullplate slices and other electronic and mechanical hardware remained on the *Hughes Glomar Explorer*.

This splitting of data is not uncommon in espionage circles when an interception is possible. It allows for protection of at least a part of the information if something goes wrong.

Late on the evening of August 16, between 9 and 11 p.m., the operator of a glass-bottom boat which provided tourist rides around the island was reported to have delivered between 130 and 135 men to the ship. He returned with about 150 individuals who had been on board. Buses were waiting for the returning 150 and their materials and, immediately upon landing, they were whisked inside and driven directly to the airport where planes, lining an active runway, stood ready for them. In as short a time as possible, they were airborne, heading back to the continental U.S.

This contingent apparently consisted of the pipe string operators, a portion of the scientific and engineering staff, most of the CIA supervisory personnel and the maritime crew.

The replacements, predominantly scientists and engineers, were the second shift, and they would be able to work on the recovered materials for more developed and detailed information, using the laboratories on board.

Only a skeleton staff of CIA people remained, and the ship's operational complement was virtually replaced.

The vessel continued to cruise the area, and used a small powerboat, leased on a daily basis, to shuttle people and various supplies back and forth to the island.

Then, one morning, the *Explorer* was gone.

It had been a strange ship, with comings and goings at night. According to local observers, no one was ever seen on deck. And it departed as suddenly as it had arrived.

No trace of the vessel's activities exist for a period starting in late August and ending in September. Sailing time for the ship, between Maui and San Diego, California, would have been on the order of 450 to 480 hours, so there are actually about 25 unaccounted-for days. Amazing rumours have been developed to explain the *Explorer*'s whereabouts during this time. One group even claims the ship attempted to recover a sunken treasure.

Since a very limited operating crew for the lift pipe system was reportedly on board, it is unlikely the vessel's systems were in use at all.

In all probability, this period was spent in running additional tests on the recovered materials and in developing more complete reports. Also, since only a portion of the clandestinely gained hardware was going to be kept, some disposal, in deep-sea depths, took place. The ship, obviously equipped for the job from a scientific point of view, was an ideal, highly secure, floating laboratory. This time was also used to repair and maintain the complex hydraulic gear and other components.

The first port of call for the ship was the familiar cove at Catalina Island. The barge, already submerged, awaited the return of the claw, and this transfer reportedly took three days. The ship then set sail again and arrived at her home berth with no further delay.

Upon reaching San Diego, an immediate and tight security blanket was slapped on the vessel and its crew.

Work on board continued for several months while the ship was resupplied, checked and had routine maintenance performed. The portable laboratories were very complete, and the availability of machine-shop facility provided the engineering and technical people with every required capability.

Finally, when the last nugget of information had been gleaned, a general cleanup was instituted. One at a time, the technical people left the ship, until finally all that remained was the marine crew. The comings and goings of many people have been reported, and one shore-based worker assigned to the vessel told an NBC TV reporter he saw crew members fill 25 large trucks with heavy equipment which might have come from a submarine. The trucks reportedly drove to Redwood City where the barge was berthed. One common denominator of the entire ship and barge crew was their silence. Even local area sailors commented on their closed-mouthedness.

The mission was essentially over. Reams of reports still had to be written, reviewed and rewritten, and engineers and scientists would be discussing and debating the data they produced for several years to come.

But we had in our possession Soviet nuclear explosive devices, their delivery vehicles, and enough Soviet code information to work over a huge backlog of intercepted messages.

The job for which the *Hughes Glomar Explorer* had been built was complete. And the ship, along with the marvellous and suspicious-looking barge, was back in port, apparently for good. One other use for the vessel was proposed, and apparently the ship did sail on a final mission.

A Soviet submarine, sometime in 1974 or early 1975, 'accidentally dropped' a package of electronic sensing devices near the Navy's weapon-testing facility off San Clemente Island, on the coast of California. The package, discovered by monitoring the sub's activity while it was in the area, was thought to have contained a sufficient assortment of gear to have recorded, and perhaps relayed, data from the weapons-testing area.

The timing of the placement of the spy bundle was appropriate, as the Navy was getting set to test the new 4,000-mile-range, multiple-warhead strategic missile, Trident I, in a series of underwater launches. Ballistics characteristics and the power of the missile would be useful in designing an effective counter-measure, and so the Soviets took the chance and unloaded their sensor package.

In the press at the time, the package was called an 'object.' It received little coverage, and was made to appear 'accidentally dropped' instead of deliberately placed.

In January 1975, approval was granted by President Ford for a *Hughes Glomar Explorer* mission to recover the bundle of Soviet instrumentation. The authorization set off a frantic race against the clock, with Lockheed workers at the Missile and Space Facility going at it 24 hours a day, 7 days a week, to develop and construct a new type of grapple.

The haste was necessitated by the test dates for the new Trident and by the meteorologists' estimate of the weather window allowing the ship to maintain station and ride out the wave-swell combination.

On April 30, 1975, the barge left its Redwood City berth and, four days later, began its submerging operation 400 yards offshore in the cove at Santa Catalina Island. The next day she was on the bottom, in 125 feet of water. Then, on May 6, the *Hughes Glomar Explorer*, which had been out for sea trials after a long period of sitting in its berth, arrived in the cove and took station over its service vessel.

The barge and the ship carried out several manoeuvres in the area for three days and then on May 9 they went their separate ways. The barge returned to Redwood City, and the ship disappeared on its mission.

All told, the barge made five trips to the sandy-bottomed, blue-water haven, and the *Hughes Glomar Explorer*, four.

On May 24, after a probable successful recovery try, the two vessels made what was to be their final rendezvous in the cove and, on May 29, the ship returned to its berth.

No one has reported whether the package was recovered, but it is unlikely the Navy would have gone ahead with the Trident I test series knowing there was even a possibility of Soviet sensors in the area. The test did take place as scheduled. So the assumption of a successful recovery is both realistic and fits in with available facts.

The number of trips to the cove at Santa Catalina Island for both the barge and the ship is important, because it indicates the only times the *Hughes Glomar Explorer* was equipped with a machine or grapple for undersea work.

The barge visited the site once, while the ship was still undergoing trials. The purpose of this trip was a dry-run test of the submergence capacity of the huge structure.

On the subsequent two visits, the submarine-grappling claw was first attached to the lift pipe string, then taken off and stored back on the barge. On the final two visits, the hardware required to handle the instrument package was put on and removed.

It would appear, then, and eyewitness accounts back this up, only two operational tasks were performed by the *Hughes Glomar Explorer*.

This conclusion is further borne out by two papers, prepared by several of Global Marine's technical staff and delivered at the 1976 Offshore Technology Conference in Houston, Texas. The papers itemize the problems and failures in the lift system and the stable platform, and give a total of only 1,500 operating hours for the Heavy Lift System, including time used for testing and refinements. This 1,500 hours, considering the months of sea trials, the fact a complete motion picture was made on the ship showing the system in action, and the time spent on two recovery sites, is barely enough to have achieved all that was accomplished. No time seems to be left for sunken-treasure recovery, missile planting or any of the other ten things mentioned by an enthusiastic press.

Final proof of this limited use is contained in a deposition, made under oath, by James M. Miles, one time captain of the *Hughes Glomar Explorer*.

According to Miles, the lift string was deployed only six times. Two of these deployments were for the purpose of 'proving' the operational capacity of the ship to the government in order to successfully terminate the contract. The remaining four uses of the string are accounted for in the recovery operation and in the pickup of the sensor package.

There is far too much correlation between the various independent sources of data to give credence to the many schemes publicly offered to explain the *Hughes Glomar Explorer*'s use. Besides, its achievements are sufficiently remarkable to stand by themselves.

It is here, however, the story takes a bizarre turn, and a series of seemingly unrelated events come together to spell disaster for the project as a secret operation.

14

A crucial point in the presentation of the original Project Jennifer proposal to the 40 Committee was the bailout technique. What would the CIA do if the mission were blown? How would the U.S. Government officially deny all knowledge of the try, and keep out of the international turmoil which would result, not only over the quasi-legal recovery of a Soviet ship of war, but over the use of the seabed as a place for an intelligence operation

The original escape proposal, as presented to the committee, has never been revealed, because it was never needed. The mission succeeded, the ship returned home and there was no worldwide hue and cry. Even the interest stemming from the original cover story about sea-floor mining died when no further news was released. Everything, apparently, was quiet.

But too many people in too many different places knew too much. News of the unusual voyage began to leak out in bits and dabs even before the ship left on the recovery try.

Some of the people involved in the project, although monitored by the CIA, began to speak to their families, who talked with friends, who in turn spoke to others about the secret deep-sea hunt. As an estimate, if 4,000 people knew something – even the tiniest bit – about the project, then within two or three years 20 times that number would have heard something. Keeping 80,000 people quiet about something is almost impossible.

Vigorous investigative reporters who knew the Washington scene began, through their contacts, to get vague rumbles about the mission and about the startling amount of information obtained. In typical California fashion, the news made the rounds of the rumour mills, shaded by personal recollection of the teller.

Two major daily newspapers, one at each end of the continent, began to generate files on the story. In New York, *Times* reporter Seymour Hersh had been working on the project since late 1973. And in Los Angeles, the other *Times* found details of the operation being brought to them on an almost weekly basis. News of these leaks filtered to the CIA, resulting, in February 1974, in a call to *The Times* by Director Colby, asking them to sit on the story.

What follows is so 'cloak and dagger' as to be almost unbelievable; but the scenario fits, and all available sources agree with it.

The CIA began to realize there was a strong possibility of a major leak when questions started coming to them from members of the press and some of the congressional aides. It was unthinkable the mission might be blown wide open before the recovery try was even made, but it appeared more and more likely as time went on. By May 1974, secrecy had reached an all-time low. But June was yet to come.

In addition to the continuing questions, which were becoming difficult to field, another governmental office provided an even worse blow.

The Securities and Exchange Commission (SEC) was investigating the Hughes takeover of Air West, a small scheduled airline operating in California and Nevada. Through skilful legal manoeuvring, the SEC was, it appeared, on the verge of attaining a court order to cause the Hughes organization to turn over to them for examination a large number of documents the SEC said would bear directly on the case.

How the SEC learned of the existence of these files and their whereabouts is a small mystery in itself. The information must have come from someone who was, or had been, high up in the now-fractionated Summa organization. The files, consisting of handwritten memos from Howard Hughes to his aides, were thought to be highly pertinent to the case.

Hughes, who had first become involved with the CIA not only for the money from possible contracts, but also according to his own quote, so the Federal Government would think twice about messing with his business affairs again, had done his work well. Secret documents were dispersed throughout his extensive filing system.

The CIA probably approached the SEC on a high level in an effort to keep the secrets hidden, but apparently it was unsuccessful. Hughes' affairs had reached the point where it appeared there would again be a public, and to him, demeaning, hearing.

Several versions exist to explain what happened next, but, in any case, these things are certain.

The SEC attained its court order demanding the records be turned over to their attorneys. The Hughes organization had some advance notice. The order arrived late in the afternoon of June 4, 1974, and that night there was a well-planned break-in and robbery of the Hughes communications centre on Romaine Street in Los Angeles, California. The files desired by the SEC were reported stolen, and the paper chain linking the CIA to Hughes was broken.

There was a lot of hubbub about the robbery and various attempts or supposed attempts to regain the lost papers, but insofar as has been made public, neither the four burglars nor the files have ever been found. Nor has any of the important information contained in the papers been leaked.

The SEC, thwarted by the robbery, continued its

efforts to serve Hughes with papers which would force him to appear in court. This is one of the factors which kept Hughes abroad for the remainder of his life.

The behind-the-scenes action which brought this all about will probably never be fully told, but exhaustive and exclusive interviews have provided enough information to offer this unofficial scenario:

There was a ready-made solution to the problem of the SEC's court order for the documents. So ready-made, in fact, it had already happened a month earlier and had helped solve another difficulty in a Hughes office in Encino, California. That office had been burglarized. If robbers were to strike again, and along with cash and other valuables, steal a large section of records, the SEC would be unable to say precisely which files had been taken. Service of the court order would be fruitless.

The next target was to be Summa's office at 7020 Romaine Street in Los Angeles, California. The modest building with 1930 architecture had been used by the Hughes organization for some years. First, in the heyday of Howard Hughes the film maker and then, in recent years, as a communications centre for his world-wide empire. Reputation held it to be a burglar-alarm-ridden fortress. Actually, the place was virtually unprotected, especially from an inside job. Or a job led and directed by a knowledgeable person.

Again, it is necessary to state no one knows what happened on the night of the burglary and in the following weeks and months. This account is based on data gained in interviews with individuals who were not present, according to their testimony, but who had 'access' to information about the incident. Only three persons have come forward in connection with the affair. Their names shall be inserted into the outline as their roles occur.

The speculation concerning an inside connection with the robbery comes from excellent sources, and Federal Judge Warren J. Ferguson, in a hearing on a legal matter connected with the break-in, issued a statement setting forth SEC staff employees' conclusions that the alleged theft may not have been one. Several officers of the Los Angeles Police Department (LAPD) have also stated the job appeared to be based on 'inside' help or information. And Richard H. Kirschner, according to a *Los Angeles Times* story, stated, in a suit filed on behalf of one of his clients, that SEC documents would 'tend to establish that agents of Hughes engineered a fictitious burglary.' The following framework fits all available facts and agrees with material anonymously supplied.

An executive-level person was given the task of engineering a planned robbery. Through an unknown leak, it appears someone with access to Summa Corporation knew, not only about the impending court order to seize the files, but also about the timing involved.

The order arrived in Los Angeles late in the afternoon of June 4, 1974. Somehow individuals involved with Summa Corporation matters knew this, and the burglary was set for that very same night. The results of the break-in prevented effective service of the order on the following day.

The person responsible for the programme had completed two jobs. First, through unknown contacts, he had hired the services of an underworld employment agent, who in turn had made arrangements with four 'experts' in the field of breaking and entering. They were ready to go on a moment's notice.

The use of a third party prevented any of the four men from knowing their real employer. To keep the third-party employment service from guessing the truth, and later using the information for possible blackmail, the instigator may have represented himself as being connected with a dissident group which had split off from the Hughes organization in a bloody round of firings and lawsuits.

The story told to the four men was perfect. They were to have a special way to gain entrance to the building. But this assistance could only be arranged on a yet-to-be-determined evening, and they were to remain ready to act with little prior notice.

The second, and easier task, was to inventory the files desired by the SEC, select from them items of a non-incriminating nature, so as to lend validity to the story later, and pack these memos, along with a few 'interesting' materials, into selected locations within the building. A certain amount of 'dirt' had to be included to prevent the robbers themselves from becoming suspicious if they read the papers at a later date. Also, the places selected for storage of the singled-out files had to look good. In other words, they had to be secure, but not so secure as to prevent entry.

Once the unnamed, well-informed planner completed his two assignments, he waited, and when word of the granted court order was passed to him, he set the wheels into motion.

Shortly after midnight on June 5, 1974, the four 'mechanics,' along with a carload of tools, were parked in the vicinity of the Romaine Street communications centre.

Although *The New York Times* reported this building to be extensively equipped with sophisticated electronic security devices, the truth is it was barely protected at all. Reports say it did not even have a working burglar alarm. Located in a seamy portion of town in an area abounding in adult bookstores, pornographic movies and warehouse-manufacturing facilities, the location depended on its imposing neo-30's design and the generally rundown nature of the neighbourhood to buttress it against assault.

It is not known if Mike Davis, a security guard watching the property, made a regular habit of walking an outside round, but on this evening he did and the four men captured him, just as he was re-entering the building through a main door. With a gun thrust in his back, David admitted the men by using his pass key.

Only one other person was in the building, on an upper

floor. Some accounts hold a second guard was present, but there is no question the night operator was on duty at the special 24-hour switchboard used by Hughes and his organization to communicate with each other on a global basis.

At any rate, the four robbers worked quietly and quickly and apparently disturbed no one during the time they were on the premises. They tied Davis and took him along while they searched out the assigned depositories.

Their directions were good. They started in the downstairs office of Kay Glenn, chief assistant to Frank Gay, one of the three top Summa executives, and worked systematically through the building. They apparently had no trouble locating a walk-in vault, a safe and the three security files. Armed with crow bars and acetylene cutting torches, they gained access to the contents. For the next four hours, using these tools of their trade, they carried out a highly methodical burglary. Fully satisfied, they neatly repacked their gear and vanished with two footlockers filled with documents.

They made a clean getaway with various papers and memos, including some of those desired by the SEC. They also availed themselves of $60,000 in cash found lying in a safe, another $8,000 found elsewhere and some saleable antiques and merchandise.

The $68,000 may well have been left by the planner as payment. It would facilitate getting the men their money without the necessity of a further contact with the Hughes organization.

On the morning of June 5, the break-in was reported. The stolen property was listed as $68,000, a Wedgwood vase, a ceramic samovar, two butterfly collections, three digital watches and one antique Mongolian bowl. No mention was made in the press of the loss of any documents.

The story made front-page news in Los Angeles, and several versions of the amount of money taken, ranging from $60,000 to more than $300,000, were reported.

Acting quietly, and still without notifying the press, the Hughes organization next, after several days, reported an inventory of the missing files to the Los Angeles Police. An immediate investigation was launched, and members of the LAPD commented publicly the job looked like an inside proposition.

The SEC people raised a real stink, and the stage was set for phase two.

A built-in red herring was needed. The LAPD, which could find no motive for the crime, had to be appeased.

The Hughes organization was probably out little money, due to their insurance. Its losses were small. But the motive originally presented to the four robbers was ransom. It was the perfect ploy.

The burglars had the files. They also picked up a little walking-around money. And they were free to ransom the rest.

Left with the materials, the four, all cautious professionals, were faced with the method of trying to collect the money they were certain was out there. They, in turn, needed a third party. Someone who would do leg work for them for a part of the loot and act as the 'collection agency' when the payoff was made. But they also had to isolate themselves from this individual. In short, they needed someone who had a record of criminal behaviour and would be impressed by participation in a 'big job.'

It is here, apparently, Donald R. Woolbright comes onto the stage. Woolbright, who was indicted for receiving stolen property in this case and attempting to extort money for its return, was found guilty of the former and innocent of the latter. His attorney denies all involvement on Woolbright's part and is said to be basing an appeal on the assertion there never was a burglary.

Woolbright, according to published reports, acquired a limited number of the stolen documents. To a man of Woolbright's experience, which includes a criminal record, involvement in a million-dollar heist and the mystery of Howard Hughes could have seemed like the big time.

On June 15, ten days after the break-in, a man identifying himself as a 'Chester Brooks' made the initial contact with the Hughes people by telephone. The voice was reportedly later identified as that of Donald Woolbright. The first call was a foul-up. The caller was not allowed to talk to either of the top Summa executives with whom he had asked to speak.

Two days later, on June 17, the crucial contact was made. The caller identified himself with the burglary.

The message was simple: There was a white envelope in a green trash can located in a park opposite 16944 Ventura Boulevard in Encino, California. (The location happened to be near the scene of the earlier break-in at Hughes' Encino offices.) 'Brooks' said if the contents of the envelope were of interest to the Hughes people, they should place an ad in *The Los Angeles Times* on June 19 saying 'Apex OK' and list a telephone number backward.

Two days later, the Hughes staff, going along with the programme, placed the ad and notified the proper authorities.

Negotiations were thus started, and $1 million was requested for the return of the documents. Several news media erroneously reported the ransom amount as $500,000, but the request was for two payments of $500,000 each. The sum, however, was negotiable.

According to *The Los Angeles Times*, the Hughes people had little interest in the files. To the police, they explained their blasé attitude by saying the documents had probably been copied; to pay for them now would only show their real importance. And set them up for further blackmail or extortion at a later date.

'Brooks'' negotiations, naturally enough, proved frustrating for him. The disinterest was clear. One story appearing at this time indicates a trusted Hughes employee, Nadine Henley, who officed in the Romaine

Street building, was supposed to have stayed home to receive a call from 'Brooks.' Instead, she went off to a party.

By the end of the first few weeks, work in the Hughes corporation was going on as usual when someone, on a routine matter, found there was an unusual document missing. A memo, not included in the materials previously known to have been taken, could not be located. A search ensued, but the results were negative. It was gone.

The memo outlined the Summa participation in the *Hughes Glomar Explorer* deal and their role in Project Jennifer. It also is reported to have indicated the specifics of the operation in some detail.

Panic must have ensued. Finally, with no other recourse, a Hughes aide went to the CIA officers conducting the Jennifer Project, and told them the memo, which could blow the operation, was missing.

The panic spread, and the upper echelon at Langley must have been in a fine state.

A question must have arisen: Was Hughes, after all these years, playing false to the CIA for some unknown reason? Was the memo really gone? Or what?

It's not hard to imagine the scene when the staff of the agency finally had to confront Henry Kissinger with the story of the missing memo.

Everyone was now faced with a real dilemma. The *Hughes Glomar Explorer* had sailed. The information about the true nature of the mission of the ship might well be in the hands of the Soviets.

The fuse may have been burning for days on the biggest bomb since the U-2. With the complications of international law and diplomatic difficulties over the seabed thrown in for good measure.

The question of cancelling the entire Jennifer mission must have been discussed long and late, and one of the deciding factors must have been the then-current attitude of Congress. An investigation of the CIA was imminent, and it would be hard to justify the expenditure of millions on a ship which, by chance, would never be used on the mission for which it was intended.

In the end, the continuation of the Jennifer Project was approved. The men on board received a refresher course on what to do if they were boarded in international waters.

The next problem was to find the missing document. Unless it had blown out a window or been misplaced, someone had it.

Judging from what happened next, no one in the Hughes organization offered the CIA any inside information, if there was any, on the break-in; but it is certain full cooperation was extended to the agency in its search for the missing paper.

The CIA's inclusion in the programme was a real bonus; it added realism to what was a very suspect story. When told of the ransom try, the CIA apparently concluded the missing memo was a part of the stolen papers and instituted an organized recovery effort.

'Chester Brooks,' in the meantime, had not been inactive. Finally, after making no further progress with the Summa Corporation, he broke off relations.

According to a *New York Times* story, Donald Woolbright approached Leo Gordon, a Hollywood scriptwriter, and asked his help in selling the billionaire's stolen files to a foreign publication. Woolbright reportedly knew Gordon because the two men had been involved earlier in a used-car deal. He wanted Gordon, acting on his own, to contact a newspaper or magazine, using the information from the files. Naturally, a payment would be required.

Gordon admits two things. First, in a published statement, he says he saw a three-page memo, handwritten on yellow legal pad paper and it related to a Hughes matter. Second, he is quoted as saying he gave Donald Woolbright $3,500 to buy one of those files. (Newspaper reports indicate the sum was $4,000.) Some mention has

been made of an attempt to contact the German
lication *Der Spiegel*, but its representatives deny
offer was ever made to the paper.

After reportedly receiving the $3,500, something h⟨
pened. Woolbright terminated his contacts with Gordo⟨
who, by this time, at the advice of his attorney had gon⟨
to the police.

The 'something' which happened was most likely the
intrusion of the CIA. Its desire to settle the case was
based on more than the satisfaction of solving a robbery.
The *Hughes Glomar Explorer* was on the high seas,
engaged in its mission. It might be a matter of life and
death.

Since the CIA had no authority to conduct operations
inside the United States, it contacted Clarence Kelley,
Director of the Federal Bureau of Investigation, and
explained the situation from the CIA's viewpoint,
including the dire implications of the missing memo.
Kelley is reported to have advised at least one member of
the LAPD of the problem to gain local cooperation.

Subsequent reports indicate the Los Angeles Police
Chief, Ed Davis, told additional law enforcement officers
about the Hughes-Jennifer-CIA deal. This eventually led
to the reported leak in January 1975 to *The Los Angeles
Times*.

The outcome of the FBI involvement was fruitless.
An elaborate scheme was concocted to trap the burglars
and their go-between, and $1 million in Federal funds i⟨
said to have been authorized to finance this plan. Eithe⟨
the programme was never fully implemented or it wa⟨
total failure.

About this time, things must have been getting ⟨
exciting for Mr. Woolbright. According to Gord⟨
statements, he had $3,500 and, since Gordon had go⟨
the police, the Los Angeles Police Department h⟨
name. Which must have been turned over to bo⟨
CIA and the FBI for further investigation.

According to reports, Woolbright sold his b⟨

October 29 and dropped out of sight. His indictment followed in March. There is the distinct possibility the SEC also wanted to talk with him about his knowledge of the matter, but no one seemed very much in a hurry.

At any rate, in March 1975, Woolbright surrendered to the police in St. Louis, Missouri. Extradition hearings were scheduled; but no one from California appeared, so he was released. Finally, in desperation, he was forced to fly back to Los Angeles on his own. He surrendered there to a rather diffident police.

The missing memo was the catalyst which exploded the whole Jennifer story.

In the widely publicized atmosphere of detente, it was very bad form indeed to be caught in a premeditated act of intelligence gathering, no matter how grand the technical accomplishment might be. The potential number of leaks, the growing knowledge of the news media and the missing memo, which was incontrovertible proof of a direct, upper-echelon involvement on the part of the U.S. Government, made detection seem imminent.

Detente was the policy fostered by Henry Kissinger. It had worked because he had worked to make it effective. Project Jennifer, due to the unpredictable reactions of the Russians, was a direct threat to that policy. Kissinger must have felt the operation was, in some degree, a threat to world peace. These feelings could only have been intensified in the tense post-Watergate atmosphere of Washington.

Kissinger's position, as indicated earlier, gave him no little control of the CIA's main line of activity, and he could, to a great degree, call the shots on specific actions. The shot is said to have been called on this one.

First, all 'official' sources were dried up. The entire Ford Administration was reportedly cautioned not to breathe a word of denial or agreement with any report of the project. In the field of international diplomacy, silence, while it may be construed as an admission of guilt, cannot be later quoted. Official recognition of

almost any kind has a habit of coming back to bite the hand which issued it.

The second required action was tougher than the first. The story had to be suppressed in the news media. Colby, as head of the CIA, was nominated the man to do so.

In December 1974 and January 1975, Colby began a series of calls and visits to the major newspapers and magazines in the U.S. But what was he going to tell them? In a way, he was between a rock and a hard place.

Congress, in an investigatorial mood, had already convened the long-dreaded committee for a major look into the affairs of the CIA. The money spent by the agency was going to play an important role in the investigation.

Colby's story had to make the CIA sound good. It had to show success. But if a success story was presented and it got out into the open, the effects on the policy of detente were likely to be horrendous. So the real information gained by the operation had to be soft-pedalled.

A line was chosen which would not make either Congress or the Soviets too angry. It also would satisfy no one.

There would be no official recognition of the project, but the operation was to be presented as a partial success. The ship and all recovery systems, upon which millions had been expended, worked as they should have. The sub, found intact, was picked up. However, the claw had been bent in the act of grappling and, through no one's fault, the shifting submarine had broken away – but not entirely. After all, there had to be some reward for the effort.

The recovered portion, however, was a disappointment because it contained nothing of any real value. The rest of the sub was still down there waiting. If security could be maintained for only a little longer, we'd go back to pick up the rest, thus giving us what we'd expended the money for in the first place.

This story appeared to have everything.

If it broke, there would be no official notice of it.

What Soviet attention was directed to it would be diverted by the foolish Americans' failure. They had spent millions, and had gotten nothing in return. It was bad of them to spy, but the end result served them right.

If the Soviet Union had the missing memo proving Governmental sanction, the failure would minimize its impact.

As for Congress, there was a bail-out clause. Yes, the money had been expended. No, the results were not as hoped. But it was no one's fault. The equipment worked perfectly. A quirk of fate intervened. But – and here's the hooker – all the hardware exists for another try.

An operation (Project Matador) was quickly established to revisit the site. This time, they'd get it all. The Congressional committee would be brought in on the secret return. They'd all be co-conspirators, so to speak.

But there would be no return, because the only way the story would be used was in case of exposure in the media. Once that happened, the State Department could step in and, waving the flag of detente, cry 'enough' to Congress.

The try for the missing portion would be prevented by the publicity of the first attempt.

It was a tidy package, because it inherently had the appeal to the news media Colby so desperately needed. To keep them silent, he had to trade on their sense of national security. Citing the opportunity to return to the site and finish the job was perfect cover. If the media exposed the story, they exposed the operation, thus making the next site visit and other future uses of the ship impossible.

Naturally, the truth – that everything of value had been already taken and the mission was a success – negated the new cover, so it would never be mentioned. The elaborate visits to influential editors and publishers commenced.

Colby, by all reports, seems to have been in an extreme state of agitation during this period, probably partly because of his concern for the mission and partly in reaction to pressure applied by the State Department.

The added stress of an impending Congressional investigation couldn't have helped either.

Whatever the reasons, the suppression effort failed.

In February 1975, *The Los Angeles Times*, with a banner front-page headline, put out a story which had been circulating through the Los Angeles law enforcement community for some time. The report concerning a submarine recovery was wrong in several aspects (it placed the scene of the operation in the Atlantic, for one thing) and carried little detail on the salvage technique, but it was a recovery story, and it was in print.

According to *The Times*, Carl Duckett, Deputy CIA Director in charge of Science and Technology, telephoned Dr. Franklin Murphy, chairman of the board of The Times Mirror Company, owner of *The Los Angeles Times*, and questioned him about the story. Murphy, who had been a member of the U.S. Intelligence Advisory Board, a group which advises the President on the quality and reliability of foreign intelligence programmes, was sympathetic but referred the matter to William F. Thomas, editor of the paper.

Later, in March, Murphy admitted having knowledge of the Jennifer Project through his service on the Intelligence Board, so he undoubtedly knew why the call was being made.

When the Deputy Director reached the editor, they discussed the status of the story and what ideas Thomas had to follow it up. When Duckett, the CIA man, heard the paper's plans, he asked Thomas if a special agent might call on him for a briefing. Thomas agreed. Subsequently, based upon what The Company's representative told him, he played down the story. Thomas, in his own words, as quoted in his paper, stated he moved the story inside 'on the basis of what he told me.'

The first real leak was plugged. The return-mission hook had held. But it would not hold for long.

The story, before it was fully squelched, was carried by the wire service run by *The Los Angeles Times* and *The*

Washington Post and several other newspaper editors became aware of it.

Colby had to move fast. According to a story in *The Los Angeles Times*, one of his contacts was Mrs. Katharine Graham, owner of *The Washington Post*. He asked her to withhold publication. Although she was impressed, she wanted to talk with Benjamin Bradlee, the paper's editor. He was out of the country, and her next referral was to the managing editor, Howard Simmons. He was only out of the building, and the two were able to meet later in the day for discussion. Her statement, as published in *The Los Angeles Times*, shows the effectiveness of the CIA appeal:

'When Howard came back, I talked it over with him, and we both agreed, and I called Colby back that day, and told him I wouldn't run the story.'

But Mrs. Graham's role was not yet through. *Newsweek* which is owned by *The Washington Post*, lacked the whole tale but had heard vague rumblings. Mel Elfin, *Newsweek*'s Washington (D.C.) bureau chief, called Mrs. Graham, according to published accounts, and was told her views on the matter. After Elfin talked with the publication's editor, Osborn Elliott, the magazine didn't run what they knew.

Seymour Hersh of *The New York Times* had also been covering the story and was ready to make a release. But Colby moved fast, and spoke to Arthur Ochs Sulzberger, *The New York Times*' publisher. Colby replayed the whole cover story, and with undiminished effectiveness it worked again. After some editorial conversation, the story was postponed.

By now Colby was going around seeing people in person as well as calling on the telephone. Like that of a man plugging a dyke with his finger, his task grew more impossible with every new threat of a leak.

Executives at the three major TV networks were talked to, and they agreed to hold their reports on the matter.

The news media, and the individuals involved in its management, showed their sense of responsibility and their patriotism by their agreement to wait until the second effort had been made.

It's interesting to note a report, which came out during this period while the second-try story was being passed around, that the huge clawlike grapple was being destroyed so as to leave no trace of the special equipment used by the recovery programme. If a second try had really been contemplated, the claw would have been undergoing repairs, not demolition.

At this point, everything looked solid as far as the coverup was concerned. But finally, the break came.

On a Tuesday night, March 18, 1975, columnist Jack Anderson broadcast the story on his radio and television shows, in spite of having been called three times by Colby. According to Anderson, Colby told him the details of the try and informed him of the numerous news organizations agreeing to withhold the information, pending the second trip. But Anderson apparently thought the CIA was merely trying to hide its embarrassment over the cost of the operation, and he went full speed ahead with his plans to air it, under the general title 'Coverup of a $350 Million Failure.'

That night, the finger came out of the dyke and the dam broke. By the end of March 1975, hundreds of stories had appeared in newspapers and magazines. Broadcast news was filled with facts and conjectures. Every known facet of the story was reported.

However, all the news media used the widely disseminated 'failure' story. To this extent, at least, the CIA's efforts bore fruit.

Worse had come to worse, and the story was out, but the cover in use was the one selected by the agency and agreeable to the State Department.

Reaction was immediate: silence from the Soviet Union, and rumblings from Congress. Officially, the Russians took no notice of the story. It was coldly ignored in their press, and no messages of indignation were sent.

Privately, it was another matter. High-ranking Soviet diplomats grumbled over the operation, the breaking of international law and the treatment of the dead mariners. However, as long as no official recognition of the project was given by our side, the Russians could make no overt complaints.

Congress, however, had different views, ranging from indignation to total delight over the announcements of even limited success. The three chairmen of the committees which had on-going inquiries into the CIA said they planned to examine the Jennifer Project, and their comments reflected the variety of outlook available on the Hill.

Idaho Democrat Frank Church, then chairman of the Senate Select Committee on Intelligence, is quoted as having said, 'If we're willing to pay $350 million to Howard Hughes for some obsolete submarine, it's no wonder we're broke.' But Republican Senator Milton R. Young of North Dakota reportedly stated the published accounts of the cost of the operation were grossly exaggerated, and he felt the mission was successful. Finally, Senator Stuart Symington of Missouri, the second-ranking Democrat on the standing Senate CIA Oversight Committee, complained neither the House nor the Senate had been properly informed on the matter.

Once it was clear the basic cover story had been widely accepted, the CIA suddenly shut up and refused further cooperation with the news media on even an 'unofficial' basis. The 'highly placed source' and the 'knowledgeable official who asked not to be named' vanished.

The silence was duplicated by every other branch of government. Still, the unique features of the mission kept the story alive. Again and again, a working reporter came up with a new angle or found another person who had been associated in some capacity with the operation and was now willing to talk. The bits and pieces began to fall together.

Colby was called in for a special Congressional briefing session during which, apparently in an effort to justify the mission and make its successes more clearly understood, he testified, according to the reports of some of the Senators present, to the recovery of the nuclear torpedoes.

All in all, things weren't going too badly for the CIA.

Then, the second phase of the coverup came into play. A concerted publicity campaign began to suggest there might have been other reasons for the development and construction of the *Hughes Glomar Explorer*. These stories caused Congress no little concern. It was hard to come out against the ship and the CIA if you were truly unsure of what it was they had done, or what they might be intending to do.

What if, for example, the ship had actually been engaged in planting missiles on the ocean floor? Or was the primary start-up vessel for a supersecret subsea city being constructed off the California coast? Or what if the ship had been designed to place sounding devices in precise locations? All these conjectures were reported, and the most bizarre possibilities were the most often listed.

This is a good place to make one vital point. The systems on board the *Hughes Glomar Explorer* were designed to lift large payloads from the bottom, not to lower massive payloads down. The systems are called 'Heavy Lift', and the hydraulics and other components are planned to maximize their 'pull up,' not their 'lower down.' There is a vast difference, from an engineering standpoint, between the two. This fact alone rules out all uses of the vessel to plant objects on the ocean bed. The task to which the boat is ideally suited is that for which it was designed – recovery of items from the sea floor.

In spite of this, the 'imaginary use' speculation continued in the press until the next unusual and noteworthy event occurred.

In December 1975, an agent in the office of the Los

Angeles County Assessor pressed for the collection of taxes on the *Hughes Glomar Explorer*. The question of more than $7,500,000 in past due taxes and penalties went back some years, to 1973, when the first questions were asked of Summa Corporation by Philip Watson, the Los Angeles County Assessor.

His logic was elegantly simple. The ship was said to belong to the Hughes interests; indeed, official documentation to this effect existed. Since its home port was obviously Long Beach, county taxes were due.

Watson's office first wrote letters of inquiry to the Summa people in Las Vegas. Dissatisfied with the response, they investigated the matter and found arrangements had been made to pay California state taxes. A lengthy legal battle ensued, culminating in an actual attempt by a staff member to serve notice of a seizure and sale-type action on the owners of the ship. The agent was unsuccessful in seizing the vessel, but reporters, who had been tipped off the attempt would be made, added fuel to the fire by giving the incident wide coverage. Through no fault of his own, Philip Watson found himself the best-known tax assessor in the country.

. The CIA was in trouble again. An admission of ownership of the *Hughes Glomar Explorer* by the United States Government was necessary to clear the legal entanglement created by the seizure effort.

Too much cannot be made of the difference between a tacit admission of participation and an official link to the government. The one would raise eyebrows; the other would raise grave international problems.

An immediate effort was launched to suppress the collection efforts of the assessor's office. Men, introduced to Watson by an FBI agent as representatives of the CIA, met with him on several occasions. They told Watson in confidence, the ship was the property of the government, but they wished it taxed as a marine research vessel, as if it belonged to the Summa Corporation.

Watson was in a difficult position. The laws he had

sworn to uphold when he took his oath of office in no way provided for this kind of situation. Finally, after due deliberation, he challenged the government's ownership, maintaining Summa Corporation was the true and registered legal proprietor of the ship.

A court fight ensued, and case No. 75-2752-R came before the Federal court in the Central District of California. Watson attempted to prove or at least demonstrate Summa Corporation's use of the ship for its own gain, through some type of undersea mining, regardless of the use the government made of the vessel. The Federal Government, taking a rare role, stepped in for Summa and brought suit to halt the actions of the assessor's office. The action was successfully concluded by the government.

But their admission of ownership became a matter of official and public record, made all the more public by the attention of the press. It took a long time for the matter to die out of the headlines. And it served to re-alert Congress to the affair. Additional hearings were convened but nothing, aside from some rhetoric about the operation's cost, came out of them.

Another force also began to make itself felt. The third-world nations, whose interest in the seabed stemmed from a desire to see it remain noncommercial until such time as an international body could be established to parcel it out for the 'good of all mankind,' began to make their own noises.

Part of the U.S. State Department's interest in the ship's mission, as has been seen, was in the area of developing both techniques and claims to support free exploration and utilization of the sea floor. Although the actual Project Jennifer activity has never been referred to in any of the international sea and ocean conferences, the accomplished fact of the mission has aided our stand on the matter, albeit at some cost of the goodwill of several of the more ardent third-world nations.

This phase of the story almost ends here, but there is an ironic twist to the climax, which is worthy of O. Henry.

The missing document connecting Hughes, the Jennifer Project and the CIA is now, according to the confession of Mike Davis, accounted for.

What happened to it? It was stolen. By whom? According to Davis, he did it. And later, when he finally realized what he'd taken, he was so frightened by the implications in the memo, he flushed it down the toilet in his home.

Davis, while employed as a guard by Summa Corporation, was on duty in the Romaine Street address on the night of the break-in. He was held prisoner until the four men left the premises, leaving him tied hand and foot. Then, according to his published testimony, he took his time in calling for help. Spotting two pieces of paper on the floor of Kay Glenn's office, he sort of scooped them up and 'jammed them' into his pocket. One paper was the fateful memo. The other was a certificate of deposit for $100,000. Then he called both the police and his immediate superiors.

Davis was later dismissed by Summa Corporation when he refused to take a polygraph test. Davis further indicates in his statement, he felt Summa was somehow unfair to him.

It's a quirk of fate and it cost many a man a long series of sleepless nights. According to a *Los Angeles Times* story, the constant exposure of the Jennifer Project in the news media made Davis nervous. He expected the matter to die down, but it never did, and day by day the pressure grew on him until he finally decided to confess. His admission ended one mystery of the Romaine Street burglary. Just as his action of pocketing the memo precipitated the disclosure of the whole affair.

Perhaps one of the worst things to have come out of the barrage of publicity on the mission is the attention focused on the ship itself.

There is, of course, no way for the vessel to be sent

anew on a secret mission. Detection would be anticipated before the ship left its moorings. What then will become of it?

The fate of the barge is settled. It, along with some of the smaller sections of lift pipe, has been transferred from whatever branch of the government holding title, through the General Services Administration (GSA), to the Energy Research and Development Administration (ERDA).

Announced plans indicate it will be used in studies to determine the feasibility of the production of electrical energy by the power generated from tidal action.

The GSA, the branch of the government charged with finding a use for property no longer needed or required by any of the other branches, was given charge of the ship. The procedures for disposing of various properties are controlled by law. If no other function of the government has any use for the materials in question, they may be given, under certain conditions, to states making application. In this case, the specific uses to which the surplus material may be put are clearly set forth in the statutes. Finally, if no state wants to file a claim, the items in question are simply sold, in one way or another.

The *Hughes Glomar Explorer*, however, is a special case.

Due to the value of the asset from the standpoint of both dollar investment and technical capabilities, an extra effort was made to find a way for governmental agencies to use the vessel. Several special high-level meetings were convened, and a study committee made feasibility reports on suggestions offered in those meetings.

No state indicated interest.

Unless some government department could come up with the necessary conversion and operating funds, the ownership of the vessel would pass out of the hands of the Federal Government and into those of private enterprise.

In this instance, the sale of the ship would have to be

carefully controlled. Obviously, no foreign government, through devious holding companies or direct purchase, could be allowed to acquire it.

The potential disposal of the vessel raised a great deal of publicity. Like everything else associated with the project, there was a tinge of drama in what would normally be a drab piece of business.

Money for keeping the ship was running out.

There has been a growing ground swell of opinion, including federal scientific advisers and key legislators, to retain governmental control over the ship. These experienced men have cautioned that the scrapping of the vessel or its commercial lease would take from the country the use of a valuable 'national asset,' one potentially employable for highly ambitious marine projects.

The original deadline for bids was extended to June 30, 1976, in the hope of finding a commercial firm or consortium of companies to lease the ship, with eventual ownership reverting back to the Federal Government at the conclusion of the contract.

The members of the National Advisory Committee on Oceans and Atmosphere, in a special meeting, agreed to write the President and members of Congress, expressing their deep interest in the vessel, and explaining why they felt it must be saved at any cost.

Similar beliefs were expressed by several Senators, including Henry M. Jackson of the Senate Interior Committee; Lee Metcalf, chairman of the Senate Subcommittee on Minerals, Materials and Fuels; and P. J. Fannin, the ranking minority member of the same group. They declared, in letters to the President and their Congressional colleagues: 'The ship could be put to use in programs designed to encourage the development of Continental Shelf petroleum resources, to recover deep ocean minerals, ... to conduct deep ocean drilling experiments, and to support ongoing oceanographic research programs.'

In October 1975, these Senators also specifically urged

the President to look into such possibilities, and in February 1976, they received assurances a special inter-agency task force had been formed to study such potentials.

The difficulties, however, in finding a use for the ship are severe. There is the problem of money to operate the vessel; costs for the crew and support systems are not inconsiderable. An estimated $2 million a year is required for this alone.

Even more important is the development of an integrated scientific programme for the vessel's use. Putting together the various elements which go into the development of such a plan is not easy, but steps have been taken in this direction.

In the meantime, the ship remains a hot issue, and the General Services Administration has held on as best it can, but it is in a precarious position. If no governmental use for the vessel can be found, and no one comes forward to lease it, the GSA is required by law to attempt to sell it. This means, in the bitter end, if there are no buyers for the ship, there might be for the scrap and salvage.

But if the GSA authorizes the scrapping of the *Hughes Glomar Explorer*, the consenting administrators could live to regret it because of the notoriety the ship has gained. Once the ship is salvaged, its unique capabilities would be lost to the world. The members of Congress are only human. They could well forget about the problems incurred in finding a use for the vessel and remember only the loss of the asset, and the fact the GSA was unable to save it. Anytime Congressional ire might be piqued by, for example, the failure of a constituent or a favourite state to obtain surplus materials from the GSA, the ghost of the ship could be resurrected and used for a club.

Or, as is certain to happen, when Congress appropriates major funding for the vital oceanographic research we will one day have to undertake to maintain our position of world leadership, at least a part of that funding will have to be allotted to the design and construction of a vessel with many or all of the *Hughes Glomar Explorer*'s capacities. Such an appropriation is bound to cause headlines about the waste of replacing a ship once in inventory with a new one. Questions will be asked about the failure to find a use for the original vessel.

There is no way, in either case, for the GSA to win. They cannot allow the *Explorer* to be sold for scrap.

The people in the General Services Administration most vitally concerned with the ship have done all in their power to find a satisfactory use for it and still fulfill the laws governing property disposal. They have acted for another reason as well.

They believe in the *Hughes Glomar Explorer* and stand a little in awe of its dramatic potential. They recognize it as being what it has been called: a national asset. They consider scrapping the ship akin to the destruction of a fine pocket watch because no one could be found to keep it wound. Somewhere, somehow, they hope funds will be developed for the further use of its powerful capabilities, and they have worked long hours to try to come up with alternatives to the scrap heap.

The June 30, 1976, bid deadline passed, and at least two submitted proposals met with some favour. Both were from a consortium of major energy companies, and the proposed use of the vessel was 'for scientific research, and, possibly, activities with a long-term commercial value.'

Another strange thing occurred, however; Global Marine, the company which designed the ship, had come forward with an agreement dating back to the original construction of the vessel, allowing the company first refusal, at whatever price other bidders might have offered, on the services of the boat. The document was a surprise to both the GSA and the bidding companies, and the matter was again thrown into turmoil.

The resolution was a decision on the part of the U.S. Navy to include the *Hughes Glomar Explorer* in its mothball fleet programme. Ownership did not, in the end, pass from the hands of the government. Another agency, dealing with maritime matters, now has full charge of the unique craft and is supposedly in the process of decommissioning it and preparing it for storage in Suisan Bay, California.

But the story has not yet ended. According to a recent statement by 'Skeet' Jones, a spokesman for Global Marine, the National Science Foundation (NSF) has granted Global Marine $75,000 to study ways to convert the *HGE* to a deep-sea exploration vessel. Other groups are also expressing interest in the ship.

15

What other tasks can the *Hughes Glomar Explorer* perform now its primary mission is complete?

To the intelligence crowd, there are other sites of sunken aircraft and submarines, both ours and theirs, plus a couple belonging to 'friends.' (When intelligence officers hold a conversation of possibilities, they almost always include 'friendlies' in their considerations. It would allow us to find out how honest some people have been, and how open our allies are in regard to operational details.) However, the Soviets expect something like this and now keep a serious vigil over the sites of their sub and plane disasters to prevent just such an occurrence.

Considering the amount of information available from a detailed examination of a nuclear-powered boat, armed with operational long-range ballistic missiles, the cost of recovery, especially since we have the ship available, would be very low indeed.

The problem of international law, though, is a rough one, and experts feel we would have a major difficulty in world courts regardless of the fact the Soviets set the precedent.

Other logical targets are the two sunken U.S. submarines, *Thresher* and *Scorpion*.

It may well come to a case of catch before getting caught. While the technology utilized in the *Hughes*

Glomar Explorer is highly advanced, the U.S. has set an example. Now that it has been done, others have been made aware, and therefore are more able to follow our lead.

Since we have executed a successful recovery, a return of the same favour by the Soviets is a very real possibility. The United States Navy has accordingly increased its monitoring activities on our various disaster sites.

Since both *Thresher* and *Scorpion* contained working nuclear power plants and live missiles, there is also the real possibility of our having to go down some day to alleviate problems stemming from nuclear contamination. The wreckage of the two ships is watched closely, as is the level of radiation in the surrounding water. Even though the problem of leakage was considered during the design stages of the boats, and discussed at length during the hearings following their loss, no one really knows what to expect in the way of contamination. It's comforting to have the ability to go down and do something about it, should the need ever arise.

But submarines aren't the only target discussed by members of The Company. There is a whole class of objects, fully legal by any definition, and recovery could be made 'in the clear,' without the need for secrecy. (It might not be as much fun, but it would be a lot less bother.)

As has been well established, the Soviet Union must test its long-range, intercontinental ballistic missiles over water, and there is the very exciting possibility of recovering the latest warhead-carrying re-entry vehicle. Naturally, these devices are able to survive the flight down from space to sea level. While most of the re-entry vehicles used in testing would not contain real warheads, or anything close in nuclear terms, one intelligence expert, who does not wish to be named, said, 'If you think about how engineers go about convincing themselves their designs will work, you would expect, at some time or another during a flight test programme, a reasonable facsimile of a bomb would be flown.' He went on: 'The Russians are known to have taken a more empirical approach to these things than we have. .... : they want to see things actually done in a test, rather than rely on dummy flights and calculations.'

Naturally, the Soviets have means on board for the destruction of the re-entry vehicle at any selected point. If they follow our lead, they have redundant systems, including a completely separate 'self-destruct' arrangement operating independently under certain preselected circumstances.

However, should such a vehicle return, and the on-board wipe-out systems fail, we have the ability, by computer analysis of the trajectory, to determine its location within a few square miles. A complete bottom survey, like the one carried out by *Mizar* over the Project Jennifer site, would reveal the exact location of every part of the vehicle.

Our engineers and technical people would welcome the recovered materials. They'd probably be grateful for even a large piece of such a device, and could produce valuable amounts of information by their analyses and logical reconstruction.

This whole subject becomes interesting when the efficiency of our monitoring system is considered. There is more than a probability several possible exploration sites have already been determined and were on a list of future missions for the only ship in the world capable of salvaging the materials from the sea bottom. As these missions need not be secret, the vessel could obtain adequate escort and guard while travelling to and from the site and while on station during the pickup. There is nothing illegal about this type of salvage at sea, although the legal aspect hasn't arisen before because no one had the capability to do anything about it.

Another intelligence use for the ship sounds like something out of Flash Gordon. Several Soviet satellites are equipped with a radio-controlled system designed to release packages capable of withstanding re-entry into the atmosphere, for recovery on the ground.

These packages might contain anything from high-altitude data on cosmic rays to reconnaissance photographs of U.S. installations of intercontinental ballistic missiles. They are known to have been dropped at least six times. These bundles from heaven contain the kind of information an intelligence system would die for. An understanding of the resolution of their high-altitude camera and film would reveal the extent of Soviet knowledge about our various bases and installations. Up to now – at least no firm evidence can be found – none of the 'drops' has fallen into the ocean although there have been persistent rumours about the pickup of more than one of these wayward intelligence bundles. Now, with the *Hughes Glomar Explorer* and information to define a general search area, such a pickup is feasible.

Satellites themselves would make an interesting recovery object. Undoubtedly they would be badly burned by atmospheric friction on re-entry. They would mainly be of interest to the metallurgists, but even this information would be valuable in determining the state of the art of other nations. Then, too, there is always the possibility of recovering portions of the electronic circuitry used in the operation of the vehicle, which could offer us insight as to its purpose and its ability to achieve its intended mission.

There are many other areas of interest to the intelligence agencies – hydrophones, for example. In a way, our Pacific network of these underwater listening posts was responsible for the construction of the *Hughes Glomar Explorer* in the first place. The detection and pinpoint location of the sunken 'Golf'-class sub were by the use of one of the most complex installations of this type of device in the world.

Under the Strategic Arms Limitation Agreement (SALT), the U.S. and the U.S.S.R. have agreed not to interfere with each other's 'national means of verification,' by which each side is assured of the compliance of the other to the established weapons limitations. While this phrase concerning verification was originally intended to apply to satellites and has not been publicly defined to include the undersea hydrophone networks, a highly placed State Department official has indicated it would, in all probability, be applicable to hydrophones deployed in a strategic manner.

Our networks, such as the early Caesar and the later Sea Spider series, would all be protected. The Russians do not have such a worldwide listening and surveillance net. They have limited their use of this undersea tool to tactical operations, such as protection for coastal shipping lines, approaches to major ports, and high-traffic, offshore intersections, where various cargo boats cross and recross each other's paths.

The recovery of several samples of Soviet hydrophones would be interesting, even though the principles upon which they are based are well known. What would be valuable is knowledge of the methods they use to coordinate the information gained from the individual units into a meaningful whole. Once we have an understanding of the principles they are using for this integration, we have the means to develop more effective electronic countermeasures and jamming. We would also be more adequately appraised of the effective range of their devices and of any shortcomings they might have in the area of deployment.

There can be little doubt, as long as the need for secrecy isn't involved, there are many intelligence uses for the vessel in its present state. A team of intelligence experts, working on this problem for a couple of months, could present many plans with excellent chances of success.

The scientific community has another list of possible uses such as, for example, the one for which the ship was ostensibly created in the first place: the collection of manganese nodules and other minerals from the ocean floor in a deep-sea mining operation.

There might be some question as to the return on the investment required to harvest these lumps of almost pure metal, but such an activity would open, once and for all, through the establishment of a precedent, ocean-floor mining as a commercial activity.

A great deal of scientific information would also be gained from the analysis of samples of a wide area of sea bottom. The vessel is fully equipped, aside from several sections of pipe which have gone to ERDA, to lower and control a machine designed to perform this function. The type of collection machine to be employed is the only question remaining, and rather detailed plans and drawings have already been made for the construction of this device. Actual undersea tractors are also available from several firms. Saab of Sweden has developed a mechanical marvel capable of carrying out innumerable tasks on the sea floor.

Another use would be to convert the vessel into a drilling ship. Two things would be required. The stable platform area would have to be modified to accept a standard rotary drilling rig. A large amount of ancillary equipment such as blowout preventers and other safety items would have to be added.

Ample space exists on board for a mud pond, so this would prove no problem. 'Mud' is the term used in the oil fields to indicate various heavy chemical compounds used during drilling as lubricants and coolants for the cutting bit. It is pumped down the drill string as the hole is made and plays a vital part in carrying away the debris created by the passage through the earth.

As a drilling vessel, the *Hughes Glomar Explorer* would have no equal in the world, and just might be the boat to carry out the long-delayed IGY plan to drill the Mohole. At any rate, with the station-keeping capacity of the vessel, it would become a very effective device for drilling deep holes into the ocean floor.

The above two modifications are expensive, and Global Marine already has a number of less sophisticated semi-sister ships to *Explorer* with deep drilling facilities in operation. None are as capable, though they are effective and get the job done. The conversion of the ship, however, is in many ways a waste and might well prove, as many conversions have in the past, the wisdom in building from the first towards a specific goal. The station-keeping ability of the *Hughes Glomar Explorer* is of a much higher degree than generally required for drilling bottom holes. And the gimballed and heave-compensated platform, while nice, is far in excess of undersea drilling requirements.

Money is another problem. A spokesman for Global Marine indicated its technical people felt conversion would require an expenditure of about $27 million. A new ship can be built from the ground up for under $40 million, and possibly for as little as $30 million. A $3 million saving might be worth-while but, in the long run, the *Hughes Glomar Explorer* would be more expensive to operate and the differences in these costs would, over the life of the drill ship, make it economically more feasible to start from scratch.

R. E. Hughes of the National Science Foundation estimated at a National Advisory Committee on Oceans and Atmosphere (NACOA) meeting in April 1976, it could take as long as four years and cost as much as $300 to $400 million to develop a scientific drilling programme for the *Explorer*. At the same meeting, Roland Reed, Deputy Assistant Secretary of the Department of the Interior, estimated the cost of refitting the ship for drilling on the continental shelf, a less expensive undertaking than deep-water hole-making, at about $5 million. He also noted he could see little likelihood of funds being made available.

One interesting suggestion, put forth by Eugene Scorsch, vice president of Sun Shipbuilding, the firm responsible for the construction of the *Hughes Glomar*

Explorer, came from the builder's parent company, Sun Oil. According to Scorsch there is real interest in using the vessel as a kind of floating laboratory to test a pilot-plant Ocean Thermal Energy Conversion System. The equipment could be installed in the Moon Pool using 5-millivolt modules of the same size as those being contemplated for a proposed 100-millivolt plant.

Conversion of thermal energy from the ocean has been a major subject of discussion in the scientific community, and a number of technical papers and articles have been written about the process. Simply stated, the plan is to pump warm water from the surface of the ocean down into the depths, where it will be cooled, and recirculated to the top again. The thermal change, as the water absorbs heat, can be harnessed to produce electrical power.

The *Explorer*, with its wide-ranging capabilities, including the portable laboratory installations and the machining and fabrication area, would be almost like having a floating scientific city built around the test installation and would provide constant monitoring of the process.

Another unusual use of the ship was proposed by a group of archaeologists and historians.

In its present form, the vessel is equipped to locate and retrieve sunken boats dating back to antiquity. The only modifications required would be the development and production of another, more specialized claw, to grapple the ancient hulks and hold them gently as they are lifted up and out of the water. Funding for this project, as wild as it may seem at first, would come from the sale of the art objects and treasure recovered in the process.

This suggestion has apparently caused no little controversy among historians, and a spokesman for the group, fearing professional embarrassment, asked to remain nameless.

'It may sound bizarre,' he said, 'but with the capabilities we understand are operational on the vessel right now, we could, by reference to old maps and documents, determine a general location and bring back enough

189

valuable objects to raise several million dollars. Especially at today's price of gold.'

The lure of gold and other forms of sunken treasure has produced some not-so-scholarly interest from several other groups as well, and at least one direct accusation that the ship has already been used for this type of activity. Charles Kenworthy, described in a recent issue of *Playboy* magazine as 'a flamboyant Los Angeles millionaire,' is, according to the same magazine, involved in an investigation to determine if the *Hughes Glomar Explorer* made a recovery try on the site of a sunken Spanish galleon.

According to *Playboy*, Kenworthy, armed with evidence on the whereabouts of a sunken treasure worth about $30 million on today's market, acquired a permit from the state of California for sole search rights in a specific area. Shortly thereafter, on August 20, 1975, the *Hughes Glomar Explorer* supposedly anchored over the very area where Kenworthy intended to raise the lost galleon. Also, according to the report, the perimeter around the *Hughes Glomar Explorer* was patrolled by other boats to keep away curiosity seekers. The *Playboy* article ends with its revelation of having found two witnesses whose testimony claims the *Hughes Glomar Explorer* did remove treasure from the site.

It is difficult to comment on such reports. There have been a considerable number of unusual, and usually unsupported, speculations about the activities of the *Hughes Glomar Explorer*. However, during intensive investigations made for this book, no supportive or corroborative evidence has been unearthed to lend credence to any of them. In fact, the business-like and efficient manner in which the project was conducted seems to make these conjectures unlikely.

Several other major U.S. companies are still studying the ship in an effort to determine possible uses.

It is hoped some means of saving the boat from mothballing will be found. At the current published costs of about $2 million a year for upkeep and docking, it won't be easy. But it is important because the *Hughes Glomar Explorer* is today's contact with the technical developments of the ocean industries of tomorrow.

16

The Jennifer Project cost a great deal of money, and when great amounts of money are spent, two things seem invariably to occur. Reports circulate inflating the number of dollars expended. It appears to be the nature of man to try to 'one up' his fellows, so the amount is subject to increasing exaggeration. It grows and grows and grows.

Then, about the time reports of the inflated amounts reach their zenith, someone comes forward with a statement on the waste of the whole thing. Or, at least, brings up the question: 'Was it really worth it?'

The dollar puffery associated with the Jennifer Project has already been discussed.

From a basic investment of about $40 million for the ship, initial reports placed the cost of the operation at $190 million. Then, apparently because $200 million was a rounder figure, it was used. In rapid succession, $210 million, $240 million, $250 million, $300 million followed. There have even been rumblings about $500,000,000 having been expended. Since it's got to end somewhere, and $500 million is a nice even figure, it will probably rest there. That is, of course, more than twice what was actually committed. But $200 to $300 million is still a lot of money.

Was the project worth it?

On balance, the answer has to be 'Yes.' Both for what was attained today, and for what will come of it tomorrow. Beyond a doubt, the operation was one of the most colossal and daring intelligence missions ever undertaken, in peace or war. And it was one of the most stunningly successful.

A phenomenal amount of information was attained, and it will be years before the full impact of the knowledge derived from the salvaged materials is felt or can be fully judged. It is likely our position in the SALT talks will be significantly altered.

According to private sources, there can be no question the Russians themselves would have been more than willing to fork over between $200 and $300 million for the same basic intelligence about our Navy. While the Soviet press has been very silent about the American coup, the high-level conferences in the technical institutions run by the government have been far from calm.

The questions being asked over there are harder to answer than 'Was it worth it?' Top Soviet echelons want to know why their intelligence people didn't come up with the idea, and why the well-publicized Soviet technology failed to keep up in this vital area. It's a good feeling to be on the side accomplishing the feat, and not on the side looking on with irritation and awe. It's not just the intelligence materials retrieved, however, which really give the mission a practical payout.

After all, intelligence information is transitory. Today's major secret is tomorrow's street talk. Yesterday's weapons technology is valueless, aside from having acted as a base for future growth. A secret process for casting cannon barrels, important during our Civil War, has given way to atomic artillery. No matter how important the information, times change, and new intelligence is always needed. This is why an undertaking like Jennifer seldom produces anything of lasting value.

But the technology demanded by the task has left us with a milestone marker of progress.

A single life span has seen man fly a few hundred feet, then leap to the moon and beyond. It has also been witness to the silent grasping of a lost artifact on the bottom of the sea.

Yesterday's three-mile-deep recovery will seem primitive in the light of tomorrow s achievements. But as with the erratic flights at Kitty Hawk, we had to start somewhere. Once we discovered it could be done, improvement followed.

Undersea, deep-down mining of the earth's crust is now a practical reality. The only thing left is to make it commercially feasible and this is being achieved at a startling rate, as we use up the more available of our planet's resources.

Of more real importance to us is the clear establishment of an international precedent, laying claim to our right to harvest the seabed. Or, at least, a vital precedent as a step towards gaining that right.

The third-world nations have not taken their international ocean-floor protection idea lightly. They want control of this, the last really unexplored territory, at least to the extent of their having a say about its disposition. In today's world, these undeveloped countries, many under Soviet dominance, have exhibited little or no love for the United States. A lot of this animosity may stem directly from past U.S. policies and may or may not, depending upon one's viewpoint, be deserved.

Regardless, the U.S. finds itself in a situation where losing out to other world interests is a very real possibility. If we fail to lead in the development of this final, ultimate source of raw materials, it will be a disaster of significant proportion to each of us.

The claim the United States has laid down will make itself felt again and again in international politics. We have created, in effect, a new position for our future negotiations.

The real decision of the nation or nations that will control this almost infinite, and as yet poorly understood, cache of resources will not be made in the international courts of law but rather on the basis of technology. The country which leads in the development of effective ocean systems will eventually reap the benefits from the sea through direct access and participation with other countries dependent upon the technology.

The *Hughes Glomar Explorer* is a dramatic presentation of the United States' level of achievement in this field. It has gone where no other controlled, man-made machine has gone. It has done what no other has done or currently can do. It shows our ability to achieve and to apply our science to the attainment of significant goals.

Sufficient facts exist to indicate major jumps forward in applied technology are often basically due to governmental involvement. This is natural, an offshoot of the growing complexity of the problems under attack and the number of people who must work in close unison on a single solution.

The ability to utilize the furthest reaches of our planet must have a higher and higher priority, because only by controlling our environment will we be able to control our ultimate destiny. The United States must assume a role on our own planet similar to the one we chose for space and apply all available technology to a study of the techniques which will enable man to work and perhaps one day live in the oceans.

The United States must become the leader in sea power, not as it was thought of in World War II, with ships of the line and guns, but through knowledge of the ocean depths. Project Jennifer has launched the U.S. in this direction.

Over all, the operation was well conceived and singularly well executed. As in every undertaking, some money was wasted, but, considering the size of the investment and the long-term return, the waste was marginal.

The actions of the CIA in dealing with the various leaks were a little heavy-handed, but the pressures upon the agency were great. Moreover, the entire matter came to a climax at a very crucial time in modern American history. Nonetheless, the operation is a viable, well-documented example of the imagination and effectiveness of our intelligence-gathering forces. They dared to dream big, and even more vital, to do big.

From the start of the project, all systems worked to their designed maximums. The spy satellites performed flawlessly, as they do each day. The complex battery of interlinked computers and communications equipment delivered on schedule. The far-flung hydrophone surveillance network fulfilled its role as our first line of anti-submarine defence. It tracked the doomed ship on its final voyage, as it tracks every nautical mile travelled by others passing through strategic waters.

USS Mizar was able to pinpoint the final resting place of the boat and to deliver bottom pictures of almost unbelievable resolution.

The *Hughes Glomar Explorer* was designed and built, advancing our deep-sea capability. The crew on board performed their task with effectiveness.

Finally, there can be little doubt the original goals proposed to the 40 Committee were more than attained. They were surpassed. Authorization for the operation has been vindicated.

When all is said and done, the Jennifer Project will stand alone in the annals of international espionage, intelligence and politics. It will be recognized as one of the most adventurous and technologically difficult operations on record.

And it was our number. We did it.

INDEX

Acoustical holography, 29
Addabbo, Joseph P., 123
Alcoa Marine Corporation, 43, 120
Alcoa Seaprobe (ship), 43, 119
Allende, Salvador, 142
American Revolution, 130
American Smelting & Refining 81
Anderson, Jack, 171
Apollo 12 flight, 32
Archeology, 189–90
Arnold, Gen. Benedict, 130
Automatic Station Keeping System (ASK), 106–7, 112, 122
Azorian Project, 6–7

Bascom, Willard N., 43
Bay of Pigs invasion, 75, 139–40
Bradlee, Benjamin, 170
Break-in at Hughes communications centre, 97, 155–65, 176
Brewster, Owen, 70
Business Week magazine, 82

Caesar Project, 16, 19

Camp Cook (Calif.), 17
Castro, Fidel, 139–40
Chile, Kissinger and, 142
Church, Frank, 172
CIA (Central Intelligence Agency), 43–4
Congress and, 51–2
cover-up by, 126–9, 167, 171–2, 173, 195–6
crew members of *Hughes Glomar Explorer* from, 87
history of, 133, 134–46
Hughes and, 75, 78
planning for recovery of submarine by, 46–63, 78–83, 87–97, 99–100
reports of lost submarine by, 23, 30
Summa break-in and, 97, 163–7
'whole submarine' story of, 23–4, 30–1, 117–20, 128
Civil War, 130
Code System, Soviet, 37, 125
Colby, William E., 48, 59, 123, 128, 142–3, 155, 167–71, 173

Congress
  future of *Hughes Glomar
  Explorer* and, 179, 180
  Hughes inquiry by (1947),
  70–1 knowledge of Jennifer
  by, 51–2, 167–8
  reaction to Jennifer by,
  171–3
Cooper-Bessemer, 55
Correa, Mathias, 136
Crooke, R. Curtis, 44
Cuba, *see* Bay of Pigs invasion

Davis, Ed. 165
Davis, Mike, 159–60, 176
Dean, Silas, 130
'Decayed' items, 17
Deep-hole drilling, 41–4,
  187–8
Der Spiegel magazine, 165
Dew Line, 16
Dewey, Thomas E., 134–5
Diesel-electric submarines
  13–14
Dietrich, Noah, 67
Donovan, Gen. William J.,
  132
Duckett, Carl, 57, 169
Dulles, Allen, 133–40
Dulles, John Foster, 133–9

Eckersley, Howard, 74
Eisenhower, Dwight, 40, 139
Electronic gear, missions to
  recover, 51, 151–2
Elfin, Mel, 170
Ellender, Allen, 51
Elliott, Osborn, 170
Energy Research and Develop-
  ment Administration
  (ERDA), 177, 187
Evans, John, 44

FAG Bearings, 55
Fannin, P. J., 178
FBI (Federal Bureau of
  Investigation), 132
  Summa break-in and, 165
Ferguson, Warren J., 157
Ford, Gerald, 151, 166
40 Committee, 49–51, 143,
  154, 196
Funeral service for Soviet
  crewmen, 125

Gay, Frank, 160
General Electric, 55
General Motors, 55
General Services
  Administration (GSA),
  177, 179–80
Glenn, Kay, 160, 176
Global Marine, Inc., (GMI),
  43, 44, 54–5, 84, 99–100,
  118, 119, 152, 180–1, 188
  description of, 78–80
*Glomar Explorer, see: Hughes
  Glomar Explorer*
Goddard Space Flight Centre,
  17
Golem II missiles, 20
'Golf'-class ('G'-class)
  submarines, 12
  description of, 14–15, 118,
  124
  nuclear material on, 36–7,
  124–6
  sinking of, 21–4
  Soviet reaction to U.S.
  recovery of, 171–2
  Soviet search for, 25–8
  U.S. cost of project to
  recover, 52–3, 192
  U.S. plans to recover, 34–6,
  40–63, 78–83, 88–97, 99

U.S. positioning of, 28–33
U.S. reasons for recovering, 35–9
U.S. recovery of, 117–29
Gordon, Leo, 164–5
Graham, John, 44
Graham, Katherine, 170
Gresham, Capt., 96

Hale, Nathan, 130
Hancock, Taylor, 43
Heavy Lift System (HLS), 110–11, 121, 152–3, 173
Helms, Richard, 46–7, 140–2
Hemming, Gary, 75
Hersh, Seymour, 59, 128, 155, 170
Hewlett-Packard Company, 35
History of U.S. intelligence gathering, 130–46
HK-1 ('Spruce Goose'), 69–71
HMB-1 barge, 80, 101–3, 118, 150–2, 177
Holliday, Raymond, 76
Holography, acoustical, 29
Hornet, USS, 32
'Hotel'-class submarines, 15
Howard Hughes Medical Institute, 65, 72
Hughes, Howard R., Sr., 66
Hughes, Howard R., 63, 64–78
Hughes, R. E., 188
Hughes Aircraft Company, 18, 65, 70–2, 75
Hughes Air West, 65, 155
Hughes Aviation Services, 65
Hughes Glomar Explorer (ship), 43, 79–80, 87, 97
  barge of (*HMB-1*), 80, 101–3, 118, 150–2, 177
  construction and testing of,

83–6, 100–5
  cost of, 52–3, 192
  crew of, 87–92, 94–5, 98–9, 116, 148, 149–50
  design of, 55–7, 89–94
  future of, 176–81
  last mission of, 150–2
  other tasks possible for, 182–91
  planning for, 55–63
  recovery of submarine by, 117–29
  return from recovery by, 147–51
  sailing of, 97–9, 105–6
  at site of lost submarine, 106–16, 147
  Soviet surveillance of, 101, 122–3
  success of, 195–6
  taxes assessed on, 173–5
Hughes Helicopters, 65
Hughes Nevada Operations, 65
Hughes Television Network, 65
Hughes Tool Company, 55, 63, 64, 66, 69, 75, 79–80
Hydrophones, 19–20, 26–7, 185–6

ICBM missiles, 16, 31
Indian Ocean, undersea reconnaissance of, 33
Infrared radiation, ship-tracking by, 18
International Geophysical Year (IGY), 40–1, 47
International law of the seabed, 48–9, 62, 82, 194–5
IRBM missiles, Soviet, 20
ITOS, 17

Jackson, Henry M., 178
Jackson, William, 136
Jennifer Project
  overall view of, 6–8, 57–9,
  154
  See also 'Golf'-class
  submarine
Johnson, Lyndon B., 140–2
Jones, 'Skeet,' 181

Kelley, Clarence, 165
Kennedy, John F., 139–40
Kenworthy, Charles, 190
KGB, 136, 137, 144
Kirschner, Richard H., 158
Kissinger, Henry, 59, 135,
  142–3, 145–6, 163, 166
Komsomolsk (U.S.S.R.), 12

Laird, Melvin, 35
Laser-beam generating
  equipment, 72
Lockheed Aircraft, 78–80
Long Baseline System (LBS),
  109, 110
Los Angeles County Assessor,
  173–5
Los Angeles Police
  Department, 158, 161, 165,
  166
Los Angeles Times, The, 19, 116,
  155, 158, 162, 169–70, 176

MacArthur, Gen. Douglas,
  132
Maheu, Robert, 76
Matador Project, 168
McClellan, John, 51
McCone, John, 140, 141
Mechanics Research, Inc. (MRI),
  35, 44
Metcalf, Lee, 178

'Mickey,' intelligence
  definition of, 130
Miles, Capt. James M., 84,
  96, 153
Mining, *see* Seabed mining
Minneapolis Honeywell, 55
Missiles
  possible recovery of, 183–4
  See also specific missiles
Mizar, USS, 28–33, 196
Mohole Project, 41–3, 187
Mormons, Hughes and, 74
Motion pictures
  of funeral of Soviet crewmen,
  125
  Hughes', 67–9
Murphy, Franklin, 169

NASA (National Aeronautics
  and Space Administration),
  54
National Advisory Committee
  on Oceans and Atmosphere
  (NACOA), 178, 188
National Labour Relations
  Board (NLRB), 99–100
National Reconnaissance
  Office (NRO), 16–17
National Science Foundation
  (NSF), 62, 181
National Security Act of 1947,
  49, 133, 136
National Security Council
  (NSC), 139
  ruling 10-2 by, 50
National Steel & Shipbuilding
  Corporation, 80
Nautilus, USS, 16
NAVSAT (Navigational
  Satellite System), 28, 31–2
New York Times, The, 59, 128,
  155, 159, 170

Newsweek magazine, 170

Nixon, Richard, 51, 75, 135, 139, 142

Nodules, oceanic, 61–3, 81–3, 187, 194

Nordburg Engines, 55

North American Air Defence Command (NORAD), 17–18

'November'-class submarine, loss of, 26–7, 30

Nuclear submarines, first, 16

Nuclear-tipped torpedoes, Soviet, 36–7, 124

Ocean Science and Engineering, Inc., 43

Oceanic mining, *see* Seabed mining

Office of Anti-Submarine Warfare and Ocean Surveillance (U.S. Navy), 12

Office of Strategic Services (OSS), 132–3, 135

Offshore Technology Conference (1976), 152–3

Orbit, number of items in, 17–18

Pacific Ocean magazine, 52

Packard, David, 34–5, 46, 49

Parade magazine, 102

Pinkerton, Maj. Allan, 130

Project Azorian, 6

Project Caesar, 16–17, 19

Project Jennifer
    overall view of, 6–8, 58–9, 154
    See also 'Golf'-class submarine

Project Matador, 168

Project Mohole, 41–3, 187

Raborn, Adm. William F., 141

Radar, over-the-horizon, 105

Reed, Roland, 188

Rickover, Adm. Hyman G., 16

Roosevelt, Franklin D., 132

Russell, Richard, 51

Saab (of Sweden), 187

SALT (Strategic Arms Limitation Agreement), 33, 58, 185–6, 193

Sark missiles, 15

Satellites
    NAVSAT, 31–2
    observational, 6, 12, 15–18
    as recovery objects, 184–6
    Soviet, 105, 184–6

Schlesinger, James, 142

Scholley, George G., 120

Scorpion, USS, 23, 29–31, 85, 182, 183

Scorsch, Eugene, 188–9

Sea Spider, 19–20, 26–7

Sea Technology magazine, 52

Seabed drilling, 41–4, 187–8

Seabed mining, 187, 194
    as cover story, 61–3, 80–3

Securities and Exchange Commission (SEC), 97, 155–61

Serb missiles, 15, 35

Severodvinsk (U.S.S.R.), 12

Short Baseline System (SBS), 108, 110

Simmons, Howard, 170

Smith, Gen. Walter Bedell, 136

Smithsonian Astrophysical Observatory, 17

Snorkels, 13–14

Sonar scanning, 28–9

'Spruce Goose,' 69–71

Sputnik, 41

SS-N-4 missile system, 15

SS-N-5 missile system, 15, 35–6

Strongback, 56, 101, 104
Submarines
    diesel-electric powering of,
    13-14
    nuclear, 16
    U.S. and U.S.S.R. fleets,
    compared, 14
    See also 'Golf'-class submar-
    ines
Sulzberger, Arthur Ochs, 170
Summa Corporation, 55, 63,
    64-5, 81
    break-in at 97, 156-66, 175-6
Sun Oil, 189
Sun Shipbuilding & Dry Dock
    Company, 80, 84, 188
Sunken treasure, 61, 190
Symington, Stuart, 172

Technology, jumps in, 193-5
Television
    acoustical holographic, 17-29
    airborne, 18
Thermal energy conversion,
    189
Theta Cable Television, 65
Thomas, William F., 169
Thompson, Capt. Elmer, 85,
    96
Thresher, USS, 23, 29-31, 43,
    182, 183
Time magazine, 46
TIROS, 17
Transit 1B satellite, 31
Treasure hunt, 61, 189-90
Trident I missile, 151
Truman, Harry, 133, 134, 136,
    144
Turner, Shelton, 73

Underwater listening and
    detection systems, 15-20
U.S.S.R.
    cooperation between U.S.
    and, on space junk, 17-18
    KGB of, 136, 137, 144
    submarine fleet of, compared
    with U.S. fleet, 14
    See also 'Golf'-class submar-
    ine

V-1 rocket, 36
Van Deman, Col. Ralph, H.,
    131
Verne, Jules, 16
Vietnam War, 140
Viking landers, 18
Vityaz (Soviet ship), 28
Vladivostok (U.S.S.R.), as sea
    base, 11-12, 15

Walker, Capt. William, 23,
    30-1, 120
Washington Post, The, 169-70
Watson, Philip, 174-5
Western Electric, 19
Western Gear, 55
Williams, D. W., 79
Wise, George, 43
Woolbright, Donald R., 161-2,
    164-6
World War I, 131
World War II
    Hughes in, 69-72
    intelligence in, 131-3
    submarines in, 13-14, 28
    V-1 in, 36

Young, Milton R., 51, 172

Selected from the SPHERE Fiction and Non-Fiction List

THE PASSAGE
Bruce Nicolaysen

In the brutal wake of the Nazi conquest of France, a group of prominent refugees flee south – for their lives. In a blood-chilling journey, they and their enigmatic Basque guide must face near-certain death on the merciless, ice-covered slopes of the Pyrenees, their only way to the border with neutral Spain.

Desperate, hunted, driven by love and fear, each must meet the ultimate challenge of survival, knowing that there's no turning back. For at their heels, like a relentless, hungry wolf-pack, follows an SS unit led by a sadistic officer who is ruthlessly determined to take them ... OR BATHE THE HIGH CRAGS IN BLOOD ...

'Fine adventure ... excitement, suspense and horror'
New York Times Book Review

NOW A STAR-STUDDED MAJOR FILM WITH ANTHONY QUINN, MALCOLM McDOWELL and JAMES MASON

WAR FICTION   0 7221 6373 8   95p

THE BENEDICT ARNOLD CONNECTION

Joseph DiMona

Three nuclear warheads stolen from an American base. And, soon after, a note to the President, informing him that an atomic explosion will take place off the coast of the USA at 6 pm on July 2 – creating a radioactive, poisonous, all-consuming tidal wave of unimaginable proportions. No demands. No blackmail.

THE WORLD SEEMS FACED WITH THE FINAL HORROR: A TERRORIST WHO WANTS ONLY MASS SLAUGHTER WITH-OUT ANY OTHER AIM OR MOTIVE.

Top Justice Department investigator George Williams has just one bizarre clue, found near the base the terrorist robbed: a 200-year-old map from the American Revolution, once the property of arch-traitor Benedict Arnold, the rebel general who went over to the British.

One clue – key to the life or death of millions ...
THE BENEDICT ARNOLD CONNECTION

'One of the best ... convincing detail and lavish imagination' *Penthouse*

Joseph DiMona is also co-author, with former Nixon aide H. R. Haldeman, of the best selling *The Ends of Power*

FICTION/ADVENTURE/THRILLER
0 7221 0499 5   95p

KRAMER'S WAR

Derek Robinson

When Lieutenant Earl Kramer crawled out of the
sea and cut the throat of a German sentry one
night in 1944, he made a big mistake. For Kramer
sole survivor of a ditched USAF bomber, was on
the island of Jersey – and Jersey was under Nazi
occupation! Trapped by the bloody conflicts of
war, the islanders' lives depended on a perilous
balance of co-existence with their oppressors.
They knew from bitter experience that any
trouble would bring instant and savage reprisal.

But to Kramer, Jersey was an irresistible target.
This stronghold of Hitler's armies was just asking
to be blown apart and liberated, and it was a
red-blooded American's duty to do it. So he
embarked on a devastating one-man sabotage
mission, aimed at wiping the Nazis from the face
of the island.

Kramer's motives were sincere and patriotic. But
to the survival of the islanders, he was as lethal
as a flamethrower in a firework factory . . .

'An original and dazzlingly controlled novel'
The Sunday Times

'Excellently plotted . . . the book moves along at
a great lick to a splendid climax'
The Guardian

WAR FICTION 0 7221 0439 1   £1.25

A MAN CALLED INTREPID:
The Secret War 1939–1945

William Stevenson

A MAN CALLED INTREPID tells for the first time the full story of British Security Co-ordination, the international Allied intelligence agency of World War Two whose work has been a closely guarded secret for the past thirty years. Here are top-level inside accounts of crucial wartime undercover operations including:

- The breaking of the German *Enigma* code
- The assassination of Heydrich
- The race for the atomic bomb
- Surveillance and sabotage of Nazi V1 and V2 rocket sites
- The raids on the French coast that made the Normandy landings possible
- Anglo-American co-operation in the sinking of the *Bismarck*
- The organization of resistance movements throughout Europe
- The intelligence stratagems that delayed the Nazi invasion of Russia

Written with full access to all the British Security Co-ordination papers and with the full co-operation of BSC's director, the man code-named INTREPID, William Stevenson's internationally bestselling book is a uniquely important piece of modern secret history. It is also tremendously exciting to read.

NON-FICTION/WARFARE   0 7221 8158 2
£1.75p

RUIN FROM THE AIR

Gordon Thomas and
Max Morgan-Witts

The nuclear destruction of Hiroshima is the most
significant single event in recorded human history
to date. RUIN FROM THE AIR tells the full
story of this literally epoch-making act of war as
never. Based on interviews with the leading
surviving participants on both sides of the conflict, diaries, government documents and a wealth
of published and unpublished material, here is
probably the most astounding book about modern
warfare ever published.

'Fascinating ... unrivalled in World War II
accounts'
New York Times Book Review

'Has the grip of a thriller'
Sunday Times

'Epic ... skilfully told ... a successful look at
one of the most significant episodes in human
history'
Group-Captain Leonard Cheshire, VC.
Evening News

NON-FICTION/WARFARE   0 7221 0494 4
£1.50p

A Selection of Bestsellers from Sphere Books

Fiction

THE TASKMASTER	Harold King	£1.25	☐
THE BENEDICT ARNOLD CONNECTION			
	Joseph DiMona	95p	☐
CHARNEL HOUSE	Graham Masterton	85p	☐
TEMPLE DOGS	Robert L. Duncan	95p	☐
KRAMER'S WAR	Derek Robinson	£1.25	☐
UNTIL THE COLOURS FADE	Tim Jeal	£1.50	☐
FALSTAFF	Robert Nye	£1.50	☐
EXIT SHERLOCK HOLMES	Robert Lee Hall	95p	☐
RAISE THE TITANIC!	Clive Cussler	95p	☐
FIREFOX	Craig Thomas	95p	☐

Film and Television tie-ins

THE PASSAGE	Bruce Nicolaysen	95p	☐
STAR WARS	George Lucas	95p	☐
EBANO (now filmed as ASHANTI)			
	Alberto Vazquez-Figueroa	95p	☐
THE EXPERIMENT	John Urling Clark	95p	☐
THOMAS & SARAH	Mollie Hardwick	85p	☐

Non Fiction

EMMA & I	Sheila Hocken	85p	☐
KINDERGARTEN IS TOO LATE	Masaru Ibuka	95p	☐
THE JENNIFER PROJECT	Clyde W. Burleson	95p	☐
THE SEXUAL CONNECTION	John Sparks	85p	☐
ELEPHANTS IN THE LIVING ROOM,			
BEARS IN THE CANOE	Earl & Liz Hammond	£1.25	

All Sphere Books are available at your local book shop or newsagent, or can be ordered direct from the publisher. Just tick the titles you want and fill in the form below.

Name..

Address..

....

Write to Sphere Books, Cash Sales Department, P.O. Box 11, Falmouth Cornwall TR10 9EN

Please enclose cheque or postal order to the value of cover price plus:

UK: 22p for the first book plus 10p per copy for each additional book ordered to a maximum charge of 82p

OVERSEAS: 30p for the first book and 10p for each additional book BFPO and EIRE: 22p for the first book plus 10p per copy for the next 6 books, thereafter 4p per book

Sphere Books reserve the right to show new retail prices on covers which may differ from those previously advertised in the text or elsewhere, and to increase postal rates in accordance with the GPO.